Activation
for
Ascension

by

David Ash BSc.

with

*The Amethyst Group
and Hillary Ravenna*

*"The Earth changes and Ascension
will lead us from cri* ⟨...⟩

Published by Kima Global Publishers,
P.O. Box 374,
Rondebosch,
7701
South Africa

First Edition June 1995
Second Edition August 1997

ISBN 0-9584065-5-3

Why not visit our website?
http://www.globalvisions.org/cl/kima

Cover design: Alan Fisher
Set in 11 point Bookman Old Style
Printed & bound in South Africa

Other books by David Ash:
The Vortex: Key to Future Science (Gateway) with Peter Hewitt.
The Tower of Truth (Camspress)
New Science of the Spirit (College of Psychic Science)

Contents

Songs for Ascension

iv

Introduction

Much has been said and written about the Ascension, and I have been travelling around the world since 1991 teaching and writing on the subject. In all that you hear and all that you read it is important to remember that ascension is basically very easy and very simple. Ascension is the opportunity for you to return home. All you have to do is let it happen for you. The very fact that you are reading this book suggests you are either drawn to the subject or are already on the ascension path. You do not need an intellectual understanding of the process - although that is helpful to satisfy the mind. All you have to do is let go and allow the process of ascension to take place.

Whatever changes need to occur to prepare you for ascension, if you chose to take this momentous step in your evolution, will have occurred or will be occurring in your life right now. Some of them will be painful. Allow whatever happens to you to occur, without judgement, recrimination or undue anguish. My suggestion is trust and breathe into each moment and event in your life as it unfolds. Let the pains and pleasures come and then let them go as you move through your own personal process. There are no mistakes. There is no set formula. Everyone is unique so each path to ascension is different.

We need to do our best to love unconditionally, live caringly and breathe consciously. Be conscious of your breath. Allow it to go slow and deep of its own accord. Stay centered on each breath because your breath will lead your focus of attention into your heart which is your gateway to ascension.

Your own trust and love, good works and care for others will lead you to ascension. Books, tapes and teachers can guide you, inform you and inspire you, but do not allow them to distract you from your path. Remember to follow your own heart and inner guidance above all. Call on your guides, and the Masters who are already ascended, to assist you and inspire you toward your rebirth into immortality. The path of ascension is the way of harmony, balance and integrity. It is not new. It is ancient and is clearly defined in all the scriptures, such as the Bhagavad Gita:

Reverence for the gods of Light, for the twice-born, for the teachers of the Spirit and for the wise; and also purity, righteousness, chastity and non-violence: this is the harmony of the body.

Words which give peace, words which are good and beautiful and true, and also the reading of sacred books: this is the harmony of words.

Quietness of mind, silence, self-harmony, loving-kindness, and a pure heart: this is harmony of the mind. (Bhagavad Gita 17:14-16)

The ascension will not happen for us as and when we expect, nor if our spiritual practice is for that end. Whatever our expectations around ascension, they will be disappointed because in order to ascend we have to let go of our attachment to everything; including ascension. The way of ascension has to be unconditional. It is not intended to be the cause of good works so much as the reward for good works.

When the moment of ascension arrives - and it will come when we least expect it - we have been told by the Masters that a doorway of light will appear before us. This is our invitation. To ascend all we have to do is step into the light. At the moment of ascension you will be alone. Your mind may attempt to distract you. Hesitation and sudden fears may arise. Then you will need to trust and take a leap of faith. In that moment surrender to the breath. It is your heart and not your head that will pull you through, so let go to love. Love yourself and others. Forgive yourself and others. Trust in yourself and your own goodness. You are worthy. We are all worthy of ascension. Live each day in love and selfless service, to the best of your ability, then when the door of light appears, 'go for it' !

Taught to believe that things are the way they seem,
We have forgotten the world is but a dream.
Accelerating change is the order of the day,
As all human structures begin to fade away.
So let the heart lead the head, that's the only way,
The mind has to know it no longer holds full sway.
For long we have wandered this Earth on our own,
Now all of heaven is beckoning us home.
Many a lifetime we've waited for the call,
Now we have to choose once and for all,
So take the leap of faith, plunge through the door,
Rise to your glory and bow to death no more.
Just focus on the breath, that's all you have to do,
Grace will lift you and love will see you through.
Its time to awaken, its time to unlearn,
Its time to let go and take the journey home.

Chapter One

The Ascension

The ascension is the imperative of our time. All other issues pale beside this clarion call to all nations and peoples on the Earth. The Omega point for evolutionary completion fast approaches as the cycle of human incarnation on Earth comes to a close. The time of harvest has arrived and the ascension is 'the gathering of the good fruit of humankind into the barns of heaven' - predicted to occur in three waves.

As the planetary timepiece approaches the twelfth hour, the winds of change blow upon the Earth, calling everyone to awaken from slumber and make their final choices - love or hate, faith or fear, joy or despair, the spiritual or the material - to prepare for evacuation prior to the cleansing of the Earth as she undergoes clearing for her transition and ascension into glory.

Humanity is awakening to such an extent that the population may be able to ascend with the planet without the necessity of evacuation and planetary cleansing. Those who are not ready or prepared to partake in the ascension could leave beforehand through the normal death process. The planet may be cleansed by advanced technologies rather than global changes. This is not just a dream. It **is** attainable.

Ascension is not for the chosen few. It is offered to everyone regardless of class, colour or creed. The only requirement for ascension is unconditional love.

1

Civilisation is a test. 20th. Century civilisation is a filter. It exists to sort out people who are ready for the ascension from those who are not. People who are not ready to ascend will be too distracted by the toys and games of the modern world to hear the voices from the wilderness calling for the ascension. To even hear about ascension, or pick up a book on the subject, indicates that an individual is passing through the filter. Then, the way the individual responds to the call depends not upon this one lifetime, but upon all their lives in their entire cycle of incarnations on Earth.

Some will heap scorn. Others will rejoice at the news of a lifetime. They won't question how it comes to them or judge its presentation. Just the word *ascension* will be sufficient to activate those who are ready. Some are ready for completion and the light body of eternal joy and immortality. Others are not. Each person will decide for themselves - not because of who they are in the world, but what they are in the heart. Under the skin there is a heart full of gold or a heart full of silt.

> *"Don't drown in the mire built,*
> *That sifts the gold from the silt."*

> (Stephen Ash, *The Puzzle*)

We are in the end times. The grand finale is given by the ancient Mayan calendar for the tear 2012. Mohammed said that in the end times the Arabs would leave their nomadic way of life and settle into high buildings and children would treat their parents as slaves. The modern prophet Edgar Cayce has also made it clear that the end times would occur in our

2

present day and age. Deep within their hearts, many people know that they are living in the last days.

However this is not news of doom and gloom - unless of course one misses the ascension! All ends are but new beginnings. The omega point breaks through like the dawn at the deepest dark. It brings with it renewal, regeneration and re-establishment of divine law. The old age of false values will crumble into dust. This is bad news only to those who are attached to it. For those who let go, 2012 is the doorway to the long-awaited Golden Age of peace, love and freedom.

The ascension is not for those seeking an escape from the Earth. Planet Earth is about to take a quantum leap in Her evolution. She is about to ascend into a new age of enlightenment and super-physical, spiritual consciousness. If you wish to stay with this, the Beloved Planet, you also have to take the quantum leap into higher consciousness.

The people of Light are now being activated to their higher calling. A new Light is emerging as never before seen on the Earth - even in ancient times. Religious fanaticism will implode; and the falsehoods of modern science will collapse unto their very foundations. Esoterica will pass as a fleeting shadow and the middling new age phenomenon will just dissipate. There is no middle ground. There is either total commitment to the light and corresponding action or a holding onto shrinking money, shallow comforts and half truths.

This is the time of the end, the end of the dramas of false action and the end of the egocentric strutting of false personas. Victory lies in humility, in the ability to release all egocentric pride and attachment. All falsehood that blinds must be purged lest it not only blinds but binds us to dust and corruption.

We are approaching the long awaited time of the return of the Christ, but know that an accounting is due upon arrival of the Christ and the Lords of Light on Earth, for all are indeed held accountable for actions and attitudes for or against Life and the Light. The scriptures of Light state that a miraculous outpouring of the gifts of the Spirit will break forth in the end times for those who are committed to service to Light and to Truth. So hold fast to your truth; which you know in your heart to be real.

As the Earth is rocked to its very foundations and the shell of materialism is shattered, those who abide in the Light, in defiance of external appearances and increasing adversity will shine with a radiance only dimly remembered and a spiritual authority such as the Earth has scarcely known. As the Earth passes into paradise men and women everywhere will rise to their true human, divine potential. It is the time when the children of God return home. If you are amongst them, rejoice for your deliverance is at hand.

As above so below, as below so above. The Universe is just like the atom, and ascension is like the quantum leap of an electron in an atom from the ground state to the excited state. Quantum physics does not allow for electrons to exist between quantum states in the atom so they can only take the quantum leap by disappearing off one energy level and appearing on another. The third dimension of the Universe is like the ground state in the atom. The fifth dimension is like the excited state. Like the quantum leap of an

4

electron in the atom, the ascension of a body from the third dimension to the fifth dimension involves their vanishing from the space-time continuum of the third dimension and appearing in that of the fifth.

An electron can only take the quantum leap if it has the minimum energy input required to lift it from the ground state to the excited State. In the same way, a person can only make the ascension if they have attained a minimum input of spiritual energy. They have to build up their 'spiritual charge' to make the quantum leap into the fifth dimension.

In Sanskrit there is a word for the spiritual charge that a soul attains in a life from their good works, acts of compassion and loving kindness, selflessness, courage, joy, clear attitudes, prayer, meditation and other creative practices. This word is 'Baramee'.

In the ascension it is not just a matter of 'going through the ceiling'; it matters 'which floor you land on'. This is determined by your baramee. On the moment of ascension it is your baramee which will decide the highest dimension you can attain to after ascension. Baramee is the level of your spiritual evolvement, which takes into account many lifetimes. It will determine your newly acquired status as an Ascended Master. It is a measure of the energy you attain in your quantum leap, so pull out all the stops. Build up your baramee by acts of loving kindness and selfless service to the Earth and to all mankind.

So, my suggestion is: don't sit around waiting for the 'lift off'. Get on with your life as though nothing were going to happen but be ready for anything to happen! Love and serve as best you can according to your own light and inspiration. Live in harmony and joy. Don't waste your time and energy in concern and worry about worldly things. Start letting go and learn to trust that your needs will be met, quite miraculously. Whilst we have to be practical and live in the material world we can give the spiritual our priority and make ready for the ascension and Earth changes - as we may well be in the long awaited day of the Son of man, when, according to the Scriptures, a major global crisis will come and then 'one will be taken and one will be left behind' :

"For as the lightning that lightens up one part under heaven, shines to the other part under heaven; so also shall the Son of man be in his day.

"But first must he suffer many things and be rejected of this generation.

"And as it was in the days of Noah, so shall it be in the days of the Son of man. They ate, they drank, they married wives, they were given in marriage, until the day that Noah entered into the ark, and the flood came and destroyed them all.

"Likewise also as it was in the days of Lot; they ate, they drank, they bought, they sold, they planted, they builded.

"But the same day that Lot went out of Sodom it rained fire and brimstone from heaven, and destroyed them all.

"Even thus shall it be in the day when the Son of man is revealed. In that day, he who would be upon the housetop, and his stuff in the house, let him not come down to take it away: and he that is in the field, let him likewise not return back.

"Remember Lot's wife.

"Whosoever shall seek to save his life shall lose it; and whosoever shall lose his life shall preserve it.

"I tell you, in that night there shall be two men in one bed; the one shall be taken and the other left.

"Two women shall be grinding together; the one shall be taken and the other left.

"Two men shall be in the field; the one shall be taken and the other left."

(Luke 17:24-36)

Whosoever shall seek to save his life shall lose it
and whosoever shall lose his life shall preserve it."

"I tell you, in that night there shall be two men in
one bed; the one shall be taken and the other left."

"Two women shall be grinding together; the one
shall be taken and the other left."

"Two men shall be in the field; the one shall be
taken and the other left."

(Luke 17:24-36)

Chapter Two

The Science of Ascension

The atomic idea, that everything is formed out of indestructable particles is a myth. Everything is formed out of energy which is nothing but pure activity.

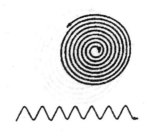

Our world is not formed out of particles **in** motion.

Our world is formed out of particles **of** motion.

Particles of motion, at the speed of light, in the form of vortex and wave...

...form photons of light

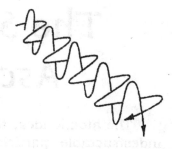

...and atoms in matter.

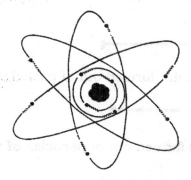

A spiral on constantly changing axes...

... forms a ball. This special vortex...

$E=MC^2$

... is how energy forms mass.

There are worlds of
super-energy formed
out of vortices and
waves of activity
faster than the speed
of light.

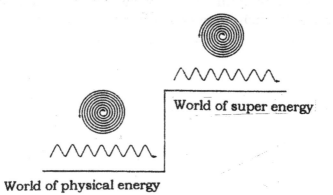

World of super energy

World of physical energy

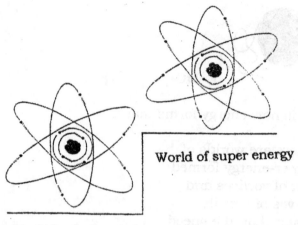

World of super energy

World of physical energy

Forms of super-energy can be identical to the forms of energy such as atoms, the only difference is the speed of activity in each wave and vortex within them.

If the speed of energy in
every vortex and wave of
a body is accelerated
beyond the speed of light
then...

World of super energy

World of physical energy

...the body would disappear from our world and appear in the world of super-energy. This is the ascension prediction.

The Frequency Error

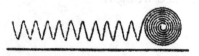

Excited state electron

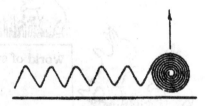

Ground state electron

There is no change in the frequency of vibration in a body of matter in the process of ascension. That would increase the temperature and excite electrons which would be disastrous for living organisms. Talk of changing the frequency of vibration is only a metaphor.

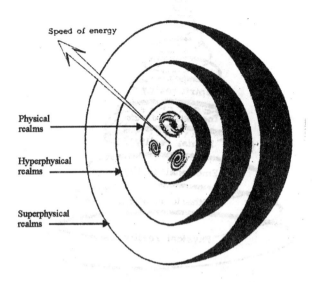

Speed of energy

Physical
realms

Hyperphysical
realms

Superphysical
realms

The dimension separating the world of energy from the worlds of super-energy is speed. As each greater speed contains all lesser speeds, so each higher world contains all the worlds formed out of lesser speeds of activity. Thus our world is but a part of a greater reality. The Universe can be represented by a set of concentric spheres. The realm of energy (the innermost sphere) is nested within the realms of super-energy (the outermost spheres). With the super-energies existing as harmonic multiples of the speed of light, this is the 'harmony of the spheres'.

15

Life

Spirit reality

The astral divide

Mental reality

Emotional reality

Etheric reality

Physical reality

The Universe can be represented by a conical vortex. The speed of activity decelerates from the apex and at each complete turn of the spiral, a level of reality occurs.

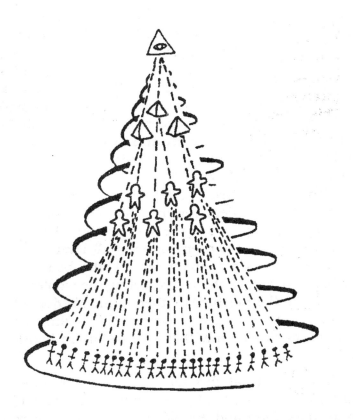

The Vortex Universe is a fractal in which the One-self branches into group-selves. These in turn differentiate into the higher spiritual selves which then incarnate into the souls and physical bodies of the lower-self beings. It is the same One consciousness in every level of self.

Ascension involves the integration of the higher and lower self in the human being. The aspiration of the Divine is to be fully incarnate in matter. The chosen vehicle for this is the human (Godman) being. This is represented by the descent of the higher-self. The aspiration of the soul is to ascend to the realm of spirit. This is represented by the ascent of the lower-self. The lower and higher selves meet and merge in the heart - the fifth level of reality. Their fusion occurs through love in the heart chakra. This reconciliation between light (spirit) and dark (matter) is represented by the Star of David and demonstrated by the Christ or avatar state of being. This is the state of true and unconditional love and the overcoming of all levels of duality. Ascension is not about leaving the body or the Earth. Ascension is about integrating the whole, in the body and in the Earth. Only then is the freedom of the Universe - in the ability to transcend time and space - given to mankind. Only then will we attain immortality.

It is crucial, at this time, that we fully integrate our higher selves into physical embodiment to prepare us for ascension and enable us to operate effectively as divine beings whilst we are on the Earth. Ascension isn't about leaving the Earth so much as being fully here as caring and loving beings. Then, instead of dying we can live with the Earth as we and she undergo the transition from physicality to immortality.

Chapter Three

Extraordinary Research

John R. Searl was an electrical engineer, employed by the Midland (UK) Electricity Board, when he constructed an arrangement of magnetised rings and rollers designed to generate and spin an electrical charge. The spin of the rollers in the rings generated and electro-motive force which induced electricity in electro-magnets set in the periphery. The generator. one metre in diameter, was first tested in the open by Searl and a friend, in 1952

To begin with, it produced the expected electric power but at an unexpectedly high voltage. This quickly exceeded a million volts producing a crackling sound and the smell of ozone.

In Searl's own words: "Once the machine has passed a certain threshold of potential, the energy output exceeded the input. From then on the energy output seemed to be virtually limitless."

Then something really spectacular happened. As the generator continued to increase in potential, it lifted off the ground and broke free of its mountings and the engine. It floated in the air, all the time spinning faster and faster. The air around it glowed pink with ionisation and nearby radio receivers were switched on spontaneously due to electro-magnetic induction. Then the apparatus accelerated off into space and was never seen again.

In subsequent experiments Searl mounted his turbines more firmly in the ground. But they still tore themselves free of the Earth, taking the foundations with them. They appeared to produce a powerful anti-gravity force and from the hemispherical crater left in the ground, it was deducted that this force was operating over a sphere with the generator at its centre. Searl had stumbled across extraordinary phenomena associated with vortex motion. He was one of a number of inventors who discovered a means of generating boundless free energy and an anti-gravity force simply by setting up spinning systems.

Michael Faraday made some remarkable but little-known discoveries with regard to spinning magnets. These have been developed by a number of 20th.Century inventors, including Bruce de Palma and Adam Trombly, into N-machines or Uni-polar generators.

If a cylindrical magnet, or a magnetised disc, is set spinning to create a magnetic vortex, at a certain threshold of angular velocity the magnetic vortex sets up an interdimensional energy portal through a "super-energy" vortex resonance. A second magnetised cylinder or disc is coupled to the first and arranged to spin in the opposite direction to damp the resonance. This simple arrangement is the operating principle of most free energy machines. In addition to generating apparent 'free energy' from tapping Super Energy sources, these vortex devices set up an anti-gravity force.

The free energy and anti-gravity properties of vortex motion were discovered quite independently by the Austrian inventor Victor Schauberger.

Victor Schauberger, famous for his construction of logging flumes, was known as the 'wizard of water'. He set icy water into spin and from this vortex motion he constructed a free energy, anti-gravity turbine.

Victor Schauberger was a young ranger in the wilderness forest of Bernerau, in Austria, when he made his first observations of the power in vortex motion.

In his own words: "It was spawning time one early spring moonlight night. I was sitting by a waterfall waiting to catch a fish poacher. What then occurred took place so quickly that I was hardly able to comprehend.

In the moonlight falling directly onto the crystal clear water, every movement of the fish, gathered in large numbers, could be observed. Suddenly the trout dispersed due to the appearance of a particularly large fish which swam up from below to confront the waterfall. It seemed as if it wished to disturb the other trout and danced in great twisting movements in the undulating water as it swam quickly too and fro.

Then as suddenly the large trout disappeared in the jet of the waterfall which glistened like falling metal. I saw it fleetingly under a conically-shaped stream of water, dancing in a wild spinning movement the reason for which was not at first clear to me. It then came out of this spinning movement and floated motionlessly upwards. On reaching the lower curve of the waterfall it tumbled over, and with a strong push reached behind the upper curve of the waterfall.

"Deep in thought I filled my pipe and as I wended my way homewards, smoked it to the end. I often subsequently saw the same sequence of play of a trout jumping a high waterfall."

Schauberger also observed that the vortex motion of water a little above freezing generated the power to lift rounded boulders, but he was especially intrigued by trout in the mountain streams. How was it they could remain motionless, as if suspended, in the fast flowing water, then dart like lightning upstream?

Schauberger was convinced that the turbulence and vortex motion of water, at it's greatest density, generated a force in the opposite direction to the flow of the stream. He believed that this force was responsible for lifting the boulders, and that trout could seek out the upstream flow of energy and use it to remain motionlessly suspended in the water or to propel them upstream and over waterfalls. He believed that trout also employed a force generated by the spiral motion of water passing from it's gills over the surface of its body.

Victor Schauberger was convinced that the conical vortex or cycloid spiral was a source of energy. To test this idea he set himself the task of building a vortex turbine based on the same principle of twisting, reeling and spinning he had observed in the fast flowing waters of freezing mountain streams. His most successful designs were based on the corkscrew shaped spirals expelled from the gills of trout, so he called his apparatus the 'Trout Turbine'.

In all his experiments Schauberger found that the temperature and structure of the water was critical as was the shape of his turbine and the materials out of which it was constructed.

In the early 1930's he fabricated conical pipes of special materials which contained a corkscrew turbine. Operated by an electric motor, the spiral turbines screwed water into a vortex flow and directed the water onto a conventional water turbine coupled to a generator. Schauberger claimed that as the water was screwed faster and faster, it suddenly began to produce enormous amounts of energy. Coupled to a dynamo, the turbine began to produce more electricity than the input motor was consuming. The system quickly went out of control as the apparatus tore itself away from its mountings and smashed itself against the ceiling. When Schauberger experimented with air turbines he found the same thing happened. Regardless of the medium, vortex motion seemed to generate energy, apparently out of nowhere, and also produced a powerful anti-gravity force.

Just before the outbreak of the Second World War a Vienna firm called Kertl were constructing and testing Schauberger's vortex turbines with a view to using them in aircraft engines. An engineer called Aloys Kokaly was employed in the manufacture of certain parts. On one occasion when he delivered the parts to the Kertl factory he was told "This must be prepared for Mr. Schauberger on orders from higher authority, but when its finished, its going out onto the street, because on an earlier test of one of these strange contraptions it went right through the roof of the factory."

An American inventor, Joseph Newman, also found that free energy could be obtained from vortex motion. His apparatus set electro-magnetic fields spinning. Newman's machine consisted of a number of rotating magnets wound with copper wire to form a reciprocating magnetic armature. According to Newman, as the armature was set spinning, an electro-magnetic force was induced and set into a spiral pattern of motion around the current carrying copper wire.

Like the other vortex generators, Newman's apparatus appeared to produce energy out of nowhere. In The Guardian March 21 1986, it was reported that in 1985, Dr. Roger Hastings, chief physicist for the Sperry-Univac Corporation tested Newman's apparatus. He found that the production efficiency of the machine was far greater than 100%. On September 20th. 1985 Hastings issued an affidavit to the effect that... "On September 19th.1985 the motor was operated at 1000 and 2000 volts battery input, with output powers of 50 and 100 watts respectively. Input power in these tests were 7 and 14 watts yielding efficiencies of 700% and 1400% respectively..."

Searl, Schauberger and Newman, working independently, all discovered the same thing; vortex motion produced free energy in apparent defiance of the laws of thermo-dynamics. The free energy machines they constructed are called over-unity machines because they operated in excess of 100% efficiency.

The experiments of Searl, de Palma, Trombly, Schauberger and Newman have not been repeated in the university establishments, nor have they been taken seriously by professional scientists on the basis that it is impossible to get energy out of nowhere. Free energy researchers have either been opposed, ignored or labelled as pseudoscientists and their apparatus dismissed as perpetual motion machines.

In 1987 Newman had his generator operating as the engine of a car built on a Porsche chassis. Started by a battery the car ran without any input of fuel. However, the American Patent Office refused to grant him a patent for his invention on the grounds that it was, to all intents and purposes, a perpetual motion machine. On the basis that perpetual motion is impossible, alleged inventions of perpetual motion machines are refused patents, consequently the commercial development of his engine was effectively blocked.[1] When Trombly attempted to patent his unipolar generator he was turned down by the U.S. Patent Office on similar grounds. Nonetheless, the U.S.Defence authorities took a court order against him and threatened him with a 10 year imprisonment for infringing secret government research into unipolar generators.

Schauberger thought he had discovered a means of 'cold nuclear fusion'. He described his vortex turbines as implosion devices. However, his research was discouraged by the Allies. Shortly after the end of World War II a group of American military personnel arrived at Schauberger's home in Vienna, seized his apparatus and took him into protective custody. What

---

[1] At the time this edition was going to press Joseph Newman had, at great expense, succeeded in getting his over-unity machine patented, and is presently looking for parties interested in manufacturing these machines. Further details from Newman Energy Products, Box 52, Lucedale MS39452, U.S.A. tel. +1(601)947-7147

they left behind was then destroyed by Soviet agents, who blew up his apartment. The American authorities forbade him to resume his research under threat of re-arrest.

The British authorities treated Searl in much the same way. In 1982, whilst he was in the middle of an experiment at his home in Mortimer, Berkshire, England, a group of officials entered the house, confiscated his apparatus and tore out the electrical wiring. He was prosecuted for stealing electricity and fined. His apparatus was never returned so he refused to pay the fine. He was then sent to prison for contempt of court. Whilst so detained his home was set on fire and most of his records were destroyed. This episode led to the breakdown of his marriage.

Another electrical engineer to receive similar treatment in our so-called 'free society' was the Austrian scientist Dr. Wilhelm Reich. Reich had emigrated to America where he attempted to develop his discovery of a means of tapping a form of subtle energy, which he described as Orgone energy. He was able to use his orgone energy devices to dissipate storms and treat diseases, such as cancer. Because of this latter discovery he fell foul of the American Medical Association and Food and Drug Administration. He was committed to prison. His books and records were then burnt and his research equipment was destroyed by the American authorities. Even though he was proclaimed as a quack and thoroughly discredited, Reich's discoveries were employed in secret research programs and he was encouraged to continue his anti-gravity research whilst in prison.

Science is supposed to be impartial, yet it allows free energy research to be treated as fraudulent because it is now beholden to government and industrial funding. Universities and professional scientists have to safeguard their reputations and incomes. Only amateur scientists like Tesla, Reich, Schauberger, Searl, Newman, de Palma, and Trombly - men motivated by love of science rather than professional status, reputation, career or money - can afford to be impartial. Financial powers, that have governments and universities dancing to their tune as puppets on strings, have made unlimited funding available for futile high energy, nuclear research to keep University physicists busy and distracted from the truth; which they prefer to keep a secret. Instead of being a tool for truth, terrestrial science has become a means to discredit anything that threatens the established, economic and industrial powers that are destroying the Earth.

The appearance of unaccounted energy in a physical system could show a discrepancy, not in the laws of thermodynamics, but in the existing, outmoded, scientific paradigm which does not allow for the existence of any realities apart from the observed physical. Because of prejudice in science against non-physical realities, circumstantial evidence is ignored, dismissed or discredited in the public mind by means of fraud.

The appearance of crop-circles is a case in point. They could not be dismissed or ignored so they have been discredited by the production of fraudulent circles. In the video of the Richard Hoagland presentation at the United Nations, *The Terrestrial Connection,*

Hoagland points out that the tetrahedral geometry in some of the circles is far too precise to be the work of hoaxers trampling the corn with ropes and boards. The formations in the crops offer supportive evidence for the existence of non-physical civilisations existing in invisible, parallel realities to our own.

Hoagland also cited evidence for the appearance of inexplicable energy in the Universe. He said that the planet Neptune is radiating more energy than it receives from the sun and the sun is producing less particle emissions than would be expected if all of its energy were thermo-nuclear in origin. Hoagland suggested that stars and planets could contain "....interdimensional doorways accessing multi-dimensional energy." He also spoke of the research of Dr.Bruce de Palma. Hoagland showed representatives of the United Nations diagrams of apparatus de Palma was using to produce energy from rotating magnetic fields, in apparent contravention of the known laws of physics.

The most significant pioneer in this field of extraordinary research was a European immigrant to America by the name of Nikola Tesla. It was hard to discredit Tesla because he made some of the greatest electrical discoveries of our age. It is thanks to Tesla that we have alternating current electricity to power our civilisation. Tesla was also the 'father of radio'. He was demonstrating coils, condensers and resonant electrical circuits for broadcasting electrical energy before Marconi 'invented' the radio. Tesla also developed a means of producing free energy and transmitting it through the Earth for everyone to tap into. Perhaps this is why he has been written out of the history books, why his name rarely appears in the annals of science and why credit for his ideas has been given to other people. Nonetheless advanced aspects of Tesla's extraordinary research were employed by the United States Government.

Dr.Alfred Bielek, a physicist and former member of the U.S.Navy, claims that Tesla met with F.D.Roosevelt in 1934. As a result of this meeting, a research project for invisibility was mounted by the Institute for Advanced Study at Princeton.

In his book The Montauk Project, Preston B.Nichols claims that serious study on the subject of invisibility began in the early 1930's at the University of Chicago after Tesla began to work with the Austrian physicist Dr.Kurtenhauer and the Dean of the University Dr.J.Hutchinson Snr. In 1933 the Institute for Advanced study had been formed to include Albert Einstein and the brilliant mathematician and originator of the tube computer John von Neumann, and in 1934 the invisibility project moved to Princeton. In 1936 the team was expanded to include T.Townsend Brown (famous for his degaussing invention for tripping mines at a distance) and Tesla was appointed director.

Tesla had discovered a resonance circuit which caused objects to become transparent. It was believed that his apparatus created a means of diverting electro-magnetic radiation around objects, and the American Government were particularly interested in using Tesla's apparatus to make ships invisible to enemy surveillance.

In 1936 the initial tests were partially successful and in 1940 a full test was conducted on an empty ship in Brooklyn Naval Yard. In that test the circuits were operated from generators on other ships. By 1941 Tesla was ready to set up his circuits on board ship and a vessel was made available to him for this purpose. He wrapped the entire ship in coils and had his famous Tesla coils and resonance circuits on board. However, as the project, code named "Rainbow", developed Tesla realised there would be problems for the crew and he became unhappy about continuing. By then, Einstein had become fully detached from the 'invisibility project' and von Neumann took over as director.

The keel for a destroyer, the USS Eldridge, was laid in 1942 and in the summer of 1943 she was lying in Philadelphia harbour. The Eldridge had been chosen for the invisibility test with a full crew on board. Preliminary tests were carried out on July 20, 1943 and on August 12, 1943 the switches were thrown to fully operate Tesla's circuits. For three to six minutes radar invisibility was achieved but the outline of the ship was still visible in the harbour. The test appeared to be going smoothly when there was a blue flash and the ship was gone.

A short while later the ship re-appeared in the harbour but there was mayhem on board. Members of the crew were found to be partially merged with the metallic structure of the ship and could only be released by amputations. Other crew members had gone out of their minds, and some never recovered their sanity. The ship was also reported to have appeared in Norfolk, Virginia, several hundred miles away.

All the evidence suggested that the ship didn't just become invisible due to electro-magnetic field effects, but rather it went through a dimensional shift causing it to vanish out of physical space and time altogether.

There is no other way to explain the sudden appearance of the ship hundreds of miles away, and the disastrous relocation of the crew into their original space-time stream, which caused them to become partially merged into the atomic structure of the ship.

The only two crew members who survived the experiment unscathed were two brothers, Duncan and Edward Cameron. They were operating the generators in the control room and were shielded from the effects when the ship passed out of physical space-time.

Realising that things were going disastrously wrong and finding themselves unable to switch off the apparatus they decided to abandon ship. They ran from the generator and jumped overboard. However, on jumping, instead of landing in the water of Philadelphia harbour, they found themselves drawn through a vortex tunnel onto dry ground.

They were inside a top secret research station, situated in a decommissioned Air Force base at Montauk Point, Long Island, New York. They were taken by security to the director who was none other than their boss, Dr.von Neumann. He was expecting them; but whereas earlier in the day they had met him as a man in his prime, now he stood before them as a very old man. It was August 12, 1983!

In the late 1940's the American Government launched the Phoenix project to research the effects of Orgone and Dead Orgone energy on weather systems and the human psyche. After the Eldridge disaster von Neumann had been moved onto the Manhattan project, but after World War II von Neumann was invited to join the Phoenix project to try to find out what went wrong with the personnel in the Rainbow project and then attempt to rescue that project under the umbrella of Phoenix.

Von Neumann and his team quickly realised they had to abandon the accepted scientific paradigm to make any progress. They had to embrace metaphysical ideas that are treated with scorn by scientific orthodoxy. They had to view the human as a subtle-energy or soul-being expressing itself through the physical body.

After ten years of research, they discovered that we are all born with a time reference point which is established at conception. In the words of Preston Nichols: "Our whole reference as physical and metaphysical beings stems from that time reference which actually resides within the electro-magnetic background of our planet. This time reference is the basic orientation point you have to the Universe and the way it operates. You can imagine how you would feel if time suddenly started moving backwards. It is this time reference point that was thrown out of kilter with the individual crewmen of the USS Eldridge and caused them untold trauma.

32

"The Rainbow technology turns on and creates what can be called an alternative or artificial reality. It creates a stealth effect (here Nichols is referring to discoveries employed in developing the Stealth fighter) by not only isolating the ship, but individual beings as well, within a 'bottle effect'.

Those beings were literally removed from space and our Universe as we know it. This accounts for the invisibility of the ship and of the people on board. The alternative reality thus created has no time references at all because it is not part of the normal time stream. It is entirely out of time...."

Nichols reports in the Montauk Project that the research began in 1948, and in 1967 a report was submitted to the U.S. Congress saying that the consciousness of man could be affected by electromagnetism and equipment could be built that affects the way people think.

Up until then, the research was conducted at the Brookhaven National Laboratories and funded by Congress. Concerned that the technology might fall into the wrong hands, Congress decided that the research must cease. They withdrew the funding and in 1969 gave orders that the Phoenix Project be disbanded.

The Brookhaven group then went to the military and said that they had a device that could make the enemy surrender without a battle simply by throwing a switch. (Nichols believes this technology was employed in the Operation Desert Storm of the Gulf War to cause Iraqi troops to surrender without a fight.

The military responded by offering the group the use of the mothballed Air Force base on Montauk Point to continue their research in secret, and they obtained their funding from private sources. The Montauk project was underway by 1971 and Nichols became assistant director in 1973.

Between 1971 and 1983, when the project at Montauk and the base finally closed down, a wide range of extraordinary discoveries were made from the research into the Reich and Tesla technologies. These culminated on August 12, 1983 with the space-time teleportation lock on the Eldridge experiment in 1943.

The researchers at Montauk were working on teleportation and they realised the importance of natural bio-rhythms. They discovered that the Earth had a natural 20-year biorhythm running through 1923, 1943, 1963, 1983, 2003 etc., when teleportation tunnels were most readily established.

The vortex tunnel, established between Montauk and the Eldridge, drew the Cameron brothers forty years into the future. According to Duncan Cameron, about two thirds of the way down the tunnel he felt an energy shift. He said there was a thump followed by a tendency to see on a broad scale. He had the sense of a higher intelligence and the feel of an out-of-body experience. (According to the Vortex predictions this would correspond to the moment when the body breaks through the light barrier, from physical into super-physical reality.) The researchers at Montauk called this moment 'the full out'.

One feature of the vortex tunnel between Montauk in 1983 and Philadelphia harbour in 1943, was that it set up an 'inter-reality vortex resonance' which fed energy into the circuits independent of the electrical generators. This is why the Cameron brothers were unable to switch off the apparatus inside the Eldridge prior to abandoning ship. They had to return through the time tunnel on von Neumann's orders and smash the apparatus to close down the Eldridge experiment.

Before the end of the Montauk project, Nichols claims that the team used their teleportation tunnels to project people to a ruined city which they discovered in the year 6037. They also used their teleportation methods to materialise an operator's thoughts. Their main operator was Duncan Cameron who had returned from the Eldridge into 1983 to work with the Montauk team. To quote Nichols: "Once they had the transmitter working, it took about another year to work out the computer programs so the system would receive and transmit all psycho-active functions. By late 1977, the transmitter was reproducing thought forms without glitches and with a very high degree of fidelity.

At this point, they pulled out all the stops. They had the psychic, Duncan Cameron (Duncan Cameron became psychic as a result of his experiences on the Eldridge), concentrate on a solid object, and guess what happened? The solid object actually precipitated out of the ether!

"In his mind, he would concentrate on a solid object and it would appear somewhere on the base. Whatever Duncan would visualise, the transmitter would transmit the lattice (or matrix) for, and build enough power to materialise whatever he was thinking of. Every single point where he could witness to a

35

particular spot on the base, at that spot an object would materialise. In other words, if he could hold an object in his hand and/or visualise it, it would appear at the given spot. They actually had discovered pure creation out of thought with the use of the transmitter.

"Whatever Duncan could think up would appear. Many times, it would be only visible and not solid to the touch, like a ghost. Sometimes, it was a real solid object that was stable and would stay. Other times, it was a solid object that would remain as long as the transmitter was turned on and then fade out as the transmitter was turned off.

The readout from the computer gave an accurate representation of what Duncan was thinking. The researchers could then select what thoughts would be broadcast out of the transmitter. Most of these thought-forms were broadcast in the vicinity of the Montauk Air Force Base, but other locations were used as well.

"What Duncan thought of as subjective reality would be created as an objective reality (either solid or transparent, depending on the circumstances). For example, he could think of an entire building and that building would appear on the base. This type of experimentation was routine."

Other reports from the Montauk project further vindicate the Vortex predictions. Duncan Cameron sustained serious brain and tissue damage as a result of continuous exposure to microwave radiation. His brain had been literally cooked by the radar waves, as though it had been in a microwave oven.

By 1986 he was certified as clinically brain dead. He continued to operate - doing such things as supporting Preston Nichols in the exposure of the Montauk Project - through his brain stem and spinal column.

This shows that the mind cannot be a mere product of brain function, as university philosophers and scientists would have us believe. Cameron's case vindicates the Vortex prediction that psychic faculties are an energy phenomenon which functions through the brain - in Duncan Cameron's case, through the surviving nervous tissue of the brain stem and spinal cord.

The Vortex predictions do raise a number of paradoxes in regard to time. The Montauk Project showed that many of these temporal paradoxes do occur in reality. Tesla indicated that if the time references on an individual are altered, the ageing process can be reversed, suspended or accelerated.

When Duncan Cameron left in 1943 to join the Montauk team in 1983, his time references dissolved and he began to age at the rate of a year an hour. Duncan's body was dying, and because his time references were lost there was nothing that could be done, in his case, to reverse the ageing process. They had to provide Duncan with a new body; and they did this by using a method commonly described as a 'walk-in'.

In 1951 a baby boy was born to Duncan's parents. With the consent of Duncan's father, the team transposed Duncan's subtle energy field - which they described as the electromagnetic signature - into the new body.

This 'soul-swapping' occurred when Duncan's younger brother was twelve, because the team had to operate within the constraints of the twenty year teleportation biorhythm.

They had contacted Duncan's father in 1947, by means of their time tunnels and explained their dilemma to him. He agreed to co-operate and he and his wife conceived the child for this purpose. The Duncan Cameron working on the Montauk project, who made it possible to set up the teleportation link with the Eldridge as a result of the psychic faculties developed through the link, was the younger version.

This extraordinary time loop worked so long as the original Duncan didn't die. The physical bodies didn't matter. All that counted was that they retained the signature or soul of the Eldridge Duncan throughout the procedure.

Their approach to Edward was even more bizarre. After 1943, Edward Cameron continued his career in the American Navy with top level security clearance, but in 1947 he mysteriously vanished. The Montauk researchers, needing both brothers in their project, had used a time tunnel to collect Edward Cameron from 1947. They avoided the situation that arose with Duncan by immediately changing his time references so that he regressed to the age of one. They then returned him through the time tunnel and planted him in a New York family by the name of Bielek. Starting life again as Alfred Bielek, he became an engineer, rejoined the Navy and was then recruited by the Montauk team as a man in his prime.

This aspect of the extraordinary research program conducted at Montauk suggests that the physical world is far more of a mind or dream reality than we in the West have allowed. This is in line with the fundamental postulate of the Vortex science that the Universe is more a mind than a concrete reality.

It would appear that time references can be reversed as easily as running a movie backwards. In a Universe which exists as an unfolding vision or dream this is no problem. Any aspect of the dream can be isolated and run in reverse sequence or transposed into a different frame of reference within the overall picture. The results of the Montauk experiments only present a problem when viewed from the standpoint of the outmoded paradigm of materialistic science and philosophy.

We have to wake up from apathy and complacence in the status quo. We have to think for ourselves. If we trust the experts to do our thinking for us, then we are asking to be treated like mushrooms - kept in the dark and fed on dung.

Al Bielek claims to have a recall of his life as Edward Cameron and his statements in this respect are relevant to the Vortex predictions. In his book on the Philadelphia experiment, Brad Steiger quotes one of Al Bielek's recalls from his life as Edward Cameron.

"I have to move back in memory to the Christmas holidays in 1941. Pearl Harbour had recently been bombed; the United States had officially entered the War; and Duncan and I were on leave in San Francisco.

"I remember being summoned by von Neumann to a secret underground facility. There was this incredible machine on steel rails. It was a so-called 'free energy' machine that was fully operational. This one small machine could produce 3.15 megawatts of power. In 1942, however, the project was put on hold, and the remarkable model was later destroyed. The 'powers on high' had declared that atomic energy would be the power of the future."

We have been kept in the dark about revolutionary forms of energy production that could have averted the nuclear nightmare and ecological disaster that now threaten our planet and we are fed on the dung of scientific and philosophical falsehoods.

In the Montauk project, Preston Nichols claimed that the experiments with teleportation and time involved technologies from other universal intelligent populations (UIPs). He also claimed that Tesla was responsible for establishing communications with extra-terrestrial UIPs, which led to the Rainbow project. He said that it was extra-terrestrial technology that was largely responsible for the success of these extraordinary research programs. He went on to claim that in these projects the scientific curiosity of man was exploited to enable extra-terrestrial entities to break through shields protecting this planet from interference from ETs. He suggested that this occurred in two ways. To begin with, the time link between Montauk in 1983 and the Eldridge in 1943 created a portal through which ET craft had virtually unlimited access to terrestrial space-time.

Alfred Bielek supported this claim. He said that when the Eldridge de-materialised in 1943 and re-appeared in 1983 it ripped an enormous "hole" in hyperspace "forty years wide". According to Brad Steiger, Al Bielek said, "This tremendous tear in time allowed a vast contingent of aliens to enter our space-time continuum. At first I thought this had just been a peculiar side-effect or by-product of the experiment. Now I understand the whole thing was a set-up."

Preston Nichols said that the second way that our planetary defences were interfered with was through a Montauk teleportation beam with Mars. In the 1970's, when the Viking spacecraft flew past Mars, it sent back to Earth pictures of pyramids and a sphinx-like face on the Martian landscape, in a region known as Cydonia. These pictures from the NASA archives are documented by a scientific journalist, Richard Hoagland, in the video "Hoagland's Mars", which was taken from a presentation he gave to the United Nations.

Nichols said that through a teleportation beam, Duncan Cameron was translocated into the centre of the largest pyramid on Mars to interfere with a very old technology left in place by an ancient civilisation. The reason for this was given by Nichols: "My personal view is that the pyramid on Mars serves as an antenna. Perhaps there is technology inside of the pyramid. He saw technology being operated there and called it 'The Solar System Defence'. According to this account, the Montauk researchers wanted this shut off. It had to be shut off before anything else could be done. This defence has been shut off retroactive to 1943, which is commonly considered amongst many UFO buffs to be the beginning of the massive UFO phenomena."

Perhaps the most detailed and authoritative account of UFO activity in this time frame is presented by Timothy Good in his book *Above Top Secret: The World Wide UFO Cover-up*. The reason for the cover-up is given by Jan van Helsing in his book *Secret Societies*. His support for the idea that information on UFOs has been suppressed in the public arena, is in pages 243-244:

'Speaking on the instruction paper, of November 18, 1952, prepared for President-elect General Dwight D. Eisenhower, on the subject of UFOs, CIA director Admiral Roscoe Hillenkoetter said:

"...On the last day the panel adopted a 'public education programme' supported by all government agencies concerned with two main objectives: educate and trivialise. The aim of trivialisation was to reduce public interest in 'flying saucers' and could be accomplished via the mass media like television, movies and articles."

Air Force speaker, Albert M. Chop said:

"We have been ordered to collaborate in a country wide disclaiming campaign to publish articles in newspapers and to give interviews to ridicule UFO reports."

Captain Ruppelt adds:

"We were ordered to keep the sightings secret, if at all possible, or, if a story had got out prematurely, to explain it away – in any case to do everything possible to remove it. If we could not find a plausible explanation, we were just to ridicule the witnesses."

Major Kehoe of the CIA said there was:

"...a cunning and ruthless censorship programme to stamp out public belief in UFOs."'

Chapter Four

UFO's and the Ashtar Command

According to M.W.Cooper,[1] between January 1947 and December 1952, thirteen extra-terrestrial craft were reported to have crashed in the U.S.A., from which sixty-five dead and one live alien body were recovered. The American Government decided to keep the escalating extra-terrestrial phenomenon a closely guarded secret and did everything in its power to discredit UFO reports and to circulate disinformation to the public. Under the authority of President Truman, this policy was maintained by the Air Force and the CIA.

In 1953, Eisenhower became President. During that first year of office at least ten more alien crashed craft were recovered along with twenty-six dead and four live aliens and hundreds of UFO sightings were reported. Then, in 1953 astronomers reported the sighting of three large objects moving toward the

---

[1] M.W.Cooper, a one-time member of the Intelligence Briefing Team of the Commander in Chief of the United States Pacific Fleet, subsequently devoted himself to exposing the extent of secret involvement between the U.S. Government and intelligent populations from elsewhere in the physical Universe. He believed that under their Costitution, the American people have a right to be informed of the actions of their government.

43

Earth, which took up a very high orbit around the equator. These turned out to be three huge space ships.

At this time a group of human extra-terrestrials made contact with the American Government. Subsequently identified as resentatives of a super-physical, extra-terrestrial group who choose to be known to us as the Ashtar Command, they warned the Americans against contact with the ships orbiting the equator. They offered protection against the alien threat and help with our spiritual development. They warned against any further development of atomic energy and made no offer of technology, citing that we were spiritually unable to handle that which we already possessed. They believed we would use any new technology to destroy ourselves. Because we were on a path of self-destruction, what we needed was spiritual rather than technological help. This they offered if America and her allies were willing to destroy all nuclear weaponry. They said we should stop killing each other and learn to live in harmony. They also warned against polluting the Earth and raping her for natural resources.

The American President chose to reject the warning given by Ashtar Command and allowed representatives from the orbiting ships to land at Edwards Air Force Base. The alien visitors were intelligent and grey-skinned. These are now often referred to as 'the greys'. The President kept the interactions with the aliens secret from the Congress and people of the United States and thus stepped right outside of his constitutional mandate by signing a secret treaty with them.

This treaty allowed for the Americans to benefit from advanced alien technology, and the aliens to benefit from human DNA to upgrade the genetics of their species. The treaty permitted the aliens to abduct American citizens for limited vivisection so long as they were replaced unharmed with no memory of the ordeal. The treaty also allowed for the aliens to operate in underground bases on American territory and for the Americans to utilise the alien craft and technology to build bases on the moon and Mars.

The truth about these bases was uncovered by a British television documentary team investigating the 'brain drain'. Their astonishing findings included an international conspiracy between the U.S.A. and the U.S.S.R. - covered by the cold war - disappearing scientists, murder, intrigue and the establishment of slave colonies on the moon and Mars. The story was televised as a documentary in 1977 and published in the book "Alternative 3". Although information about the clandestine operations with aliens was beginning to leak, it continued to be the most closely guarded secret in American history. Cooper claimed that when President Kennedy declared that he was going to tell Congress and the people, he was prevented from doing so by his assassination.

He also tells another extraordinary story. Because the alien liaison was withheld from Congress, funding was a major problem. This was overcome in the 1960's by siphoning money from the space program, but in the 1970's money was raised through the CIA by importing drugs from South America via oil platforms off the Texan coast. Cooper then claimed that the oil executive who sanctioned this drug smuggling operation went on to become President of the United States.

After the rebuff by the American Government, the Ashtar Command spoke directly to the people of America by superimposing a spoken message over television and radio broadcasts. They then repeated this procedure in other countries.

In England, for example, the Ashtar Command broke in on a phone-in radio programme. This 'E.T. phone Earth' occurred on January 8th. 1971 whilst Rex Dutta was broadcasting. The conversation with the Ashtar Command was recorded and the transcript was published in 1972 in Rex Dutta's book "Flying Saucer Message". The Ashtar Command also spoke over the early evening television news in South East England. This occurred on 26th. November 1977. Five transmitters had been 'taken over' simultaneously so that the voice was heard by viewers in London and the South East, from Southampton to Kent. Television engineers were unable to trace the voice, suppress it or stop it and all their instruments indicated normal transmission was in progress. The IBA tried to assure viewers the incident was a hoax and were reluctant to release more than thirty seconds of the recorded message.

However, thanks to a report in "New Life Magazine" a tape recording of the message, in full, was obtained by Rex Dutta and published in the January 1978 issue of his monthly newsletter "Viewpoint

Aquarius". Many viewers recall this extraordinary incident.

It was 6.12 p.m. and Ivor Mills was the newscaster on ITV Southern television. His face was visible, but his voice was replaced for five and a half minutes by the voice of a representative of the Ashtar Command saying:

"We speak to you now in peace and wisdom, as we have done to your brothers and sisters all over your planet Earth. We come to warn you of the destiny of your race and your world, so that you may communicate to your fellow beings the course you must take to avoid the disasters which threaten your world, and the beings in our worlds around you. This is in order that you may share in the great awakening as the planet passes into the New Age of Aquarius. The New Age can be a time of great peace and evolution for your race, but only if your rulers are made aware of the evil forces that can overshadow their judgements.

"Be still now and listen, for your chance may not come again. For many years your scientists, governments and generals have not heeded our warnings. They have continued to experiment with the evil forces of what you call nuclear energy. Atomic bombs can destroy the Earth, and the beings of your sister worlds, in a moment. The wastes from atomic power systems will poison your planet for many thousands of your years to come. We, who have followed the path of evolution for far longer than you, have long since realised that atomic energy is always directed against life. It has no peaceful application. Its use, and research into its use,

47

must be ceased at once, or you all risk destruction. All weapons of evil must be removed.

"The time of conflict is now past. The race, of which you are a part, may proceed to the highest planes of evolution, if you show yourselves worthy to do so. You have but a short time to learn to live together in peace and goodwill. Small groups, all over the planet, are learning this and exist to pass on the light of the dawning New Age to you all. You are free to accept or reject their teachings, but only those who learn to live in peace will pass to the higher realms of spiritual evolution.

"Be aware also, that there are many false prophets and guides operating in your world. They will suck your energy from you - the energy you call money - and will put it to evil ends, giving you worthless dross in return. Your inner divine self will protect you from this. You must learn to be sensitive to the voice within that can tell you what is truth, and what is confusion, chaos and untruth. Learn to listen to the voice of truth which is within you, and you will lead yourselves onto the path of evolution.

"This is our message to our dear friends. We have watched you growing for many years, as you too have watched our lights in your skies. You know now that we are here, and that there are more beings on and around your Earth than your scientists admit. We are deeply concerned about you and your path towards the light, and will do all we can to help you. Have no fear. Seek only to know yourselves and live in harmony with the ways of your planet Earth.

"We of the Ashtar Galactic Command thank you for your attention. We are now leaving the planes of your

48

existence. May you be blessed by the supreme love and truth of the Cosmos."

The Ashtar Command also resorted to channelling information through private individuals. Although channelled information has to be treated with considerable discretion, the messages coming through the Ashtar Command channellings are especially relevant as they include predictions of physical ascension, consistent with the vortex predictions in my own book "The Vortex: Key to Future Science", for shifting matter in and out of space-time.

The prediction of ascension was not confined to my vortex physics and the Ashtar Command channellings. A similar message was coming from other, completely independent sources. On the 2nd. and 3rd. January 1973, James Hurtak PhD. had been taken out of physical space and time by means of the ascension process, and was given "The Book of Knowledge: The 64 Keys of Enoch" The prediction of ascension was central to this scriptural science and the fact that Hurtak was not linked with the Ashtar Command offered corroboration for the ascension message.

Robert Coon from Glastonbury also offered independent verification for the ascension message. He had been promulgating the idea of planetary ascension and physical immortality for many years, and like Hurtak, he had no connection with channellings and the Ashtar Command. Solara, from America was also predicting ascension in association with her 11:11 programme.

Solara pointed to the 11th.January, 1992 as a trigger date. She toured the world, calling on people to participate in her 11:11 celebrations on that day. This was important she said, in order to open the gateway to ascension. Thousands of people responded and formed a network from Egypt to New Zealand and from England to Australia and America, to dance the symbolic 'wheels whithin wheels' and celebrate the beginning of a twenty year period during which ascension would occur for the Earth and her inhabitants. She gave the year 2011 as the year when the ascension of the Earth and her inhabitants would be complete.

In early 1979, Ken Carey received the *Starseed Transmissions* which gave the year 2011 as the date for the 'Second Coming of Christ'. This date is also given in unconfirmed reports of the *Third Secret of Fatima,* as the time of the second coming. In the Ken Carey channellings, this event is given as the awakening of humanity to it's inate divinity, the coming of millions of individuals to their Christhood rather than the return of a single, individual Christ to Earth. Ken Carey describes the accelerated awakening of humanity to Spirit as an ascent of mankind toward Spirit and a descent of Spirit into man, culminating in the dawn of a new age, the Kingdom of Heaven on Earth, in 2011.

However, in my opinion, the most outstanding channellings of the predictions for Ascension began to occur in 1990 though Eric Klein, a channel living in Santa Cruz, California. In february 1990, half a dozen people made their way to a house on the outskirts of

50

Santa Cruz in California. It was early evening and the thunder of freeway traffic filled the air. neither the house nor its surrounds gave a hint of what was about to happen. Eric Klein greeted the people warmly as they arrived. There was nothing unusual about him or his acupuncturist wife, Christine; nothing to suggest the revelation about to occur through them.

At 8.00 pm, Eric set up a tape recorder and settled into meditation. Christine sat next to him and closed her eyes. People were still coming in from the kitchen, but as the chatter died away and everyone began to meditate, a presence filled the Klein's living room. Eric coughed a couple of times and began to speak. "Hello, nice to be here with you this evening on this auspicious occasion. I am Jesus...."

Eric started conscious channelling of the Christ and other Ascended Masters in 1986. From 1988 onwards, he began public channellings and held regular, weekly evening gatherings at his home. In January 1990 he was asked by the Christ to channel a course on the topic of ascension. This occurred over a six week period, commencing in February 1990. Eric recorded the course, and his resonant voice - backed by traffic noise, squeaking doors and telephones ringing - was captured on five C90 cassettes. The impact of those recordings - first known as "the Ascension Tapes" and then simply as "The Tapes" - was staggering. Thousands of networkers throughout the world were galvanised into action. The tapes were copied again and again until the voice was only just discernable above hiss. By 1993 they were reaching hundreds of thousands of people. The global brain

51

was firing as if it had received an electric shock. Ascension fever passed from America to Australia and New Zealand and then back to England and from the triangle between those countries, it spread world-wide as people from Europe to India and the Far East to South America and Eastern Europe to Africa began to wake up to the ascension message. Some were incredulous and others outraged but most were ecstatic - for them, the prediction of ascension was the best news they had ever heard.

Eric was not alone. Other channels had received information about the ascension; some of them decades before. Godfrey Ray King had received information from Ascended Masters in the 1930's and Sister Thedra was receiving information about the possibility of ascension in the 1950's. These were corroberated in the 1960's and 70's by the Mark Age channellings. In the 1980's, the publications on ascension by Tuella and Mark Prophet added to the available information on ascension but the floodgates really opened in 1990. Along with the Klein tapes, transcripts of ascension messages channelled through Ariana Sheran of Cloverleaf Connections in Canada, through Crea of the Wings of Light and Tuieta of the Portals of Light, were circulating and in America a World Ascension Network was established.

In 1990, the amazing book *ET 101* was published in America and in 1991, Chrissie Romano of the Crystalview Sanctuary in Australia was also recieving messages about ascension. These were all being networked, alongside the scores of follow-on tapes from Eric Klein, Crea and Ariana. People all over the globe are now listening to these new teachings of the Ascended Masters - of which the Eric Klein channelings are renowned for their clarity, humour and simplicity.

In the ascension channelings, especially those of Eric Klein, we have one of the greatest treasuries of wisdom teaching available on Earth today. According to the Eric Klein channellings, the Ashtar Command is a task force operating, in the fifth dimension, for a super-physical group of beings known as the Great White Brotherhood.

Many members of the Great White Brotherhood have been incarnate on the Earth as leaders, teachers and healers and are known amongst their peers by different names to those given on Earth. The Ashtar Command is currently employed to ascend the Earth, along with its people and other life forms, by the one known as Sananda. He is supreme commander of this particular ascension operation. Sananda came to the Earth two thousand years ago as Jesus the Christ. The Command itself is headed by another being of comparable stature called Ashtar. He is a specialist on the ascension process and is working alongside Sananda as co-ordinator and technical adviser in the awesome process of ascending a planet and its population.

According to all the ascension predictions, we are coming to the end of a cycle. The Earth is destined to ascend, but because we are destroying her, there cannot be any further delay in this next step of the planet's evolution. We have the choice to ascend with the Earth or remain behind in the physical Universe and continue in the cycle of birth and death on other planets.

If we wish to ascend, we will be given three opportunities, described as the three waves of ascension. These, and the subsequent 'cleansing of the planet' - prior to her ascension and recreation - are predicted to occur before the end of the year 2012.

The first wave of ascension, anticipated to number in thousands, was expected to occur before 1996. However, with the resolution of the Balkans conflict - the fact that it did not escalate into world war in 1995 - the anticipated emergency requiring the beginning of the ascension programme at that time, passed. The waves of ascension are not now expected to begin before the end of this decade.

At Medjugorie, in the former Yugoslavia, the Blessed Mother Mary said that a long time ago Satan asked permission to test the faith of humanity for a century. He was offered any century he chose and allowed to use any means he chose to test the spiritual worth of the people of Earth. Apparently he chose the 20th.Century! In line with this information, ascension - which is the graduation and triumph from this test - will only occur at the end of that period unless an emergency such as a nuclear conflict, necessitates it occurring sooner. As the flash points of the Gulf War and the Balkan conflict have passed without a nuclear threat arising, the test of Satan, so essential to the evolvement of humanity in preparation for ascension, can run its allotted course.

"Lucifer is the archangel whose job it is to hone the souls of spirits and through difficulty challenge and adversity to prepare them for the Light or Diamond Body"[2]

In the ascension tapes, Sananda presents himself as a human being who took the step of ascension at the end of his life on Earth. In doing so he paved the way for mass human ascension at this time. He said that his special task is to help us make the quantum leap into the fifth dimension and beyond. He assures us, from his own experience, that those who ascend will neither grow old, suffer disease or any of the other limitations that are so much a part of physical life on Earth. He has emphasised that ascension - normally a rare opportunity - is now available to every human being on the planet, regardless of colour, class or creed.

It is a free gift available to anyone with a loving heart, free of fear and anger, who is willing to give it priority in their lives. Along with a sincere desire to ascend, there needs to be a willingness to love oneself and others unconditionally, with an attitude of detachment from the things of this world. There should also be an appreciation and respect for the Creator, regardless of what the Creator is perceived to be.

The suggested way to prepare for ascension is the practice of 'inner quiet' for which the stilling of the mind, by focussing on the breath, is strongly recommended. Sananda has outlined that either ascension,

---

[2] "The Only Planet of Choice" by Schlemmer and Jenkins, Gateway Books

or physical evacuation, for all innocents, children, and adults of the right disposition who will allow it to happen to them, will occur. He stressed that people do not have to be religious in order to ascend, but rather they need to be trusting, loving and fearless. The Klein tapes explain that when ascension occurs, it will be without warning. There will be the sudden appearance of an opening of light, which could occur in a sleeping or awakened state. In order to ascend, the individual has to simply step into the light.

Members of the Ashtar Command will employ organic, fifth-dimensional bodies in the ascension process. These are described in the Keys of Enoch as Merkabah. The Merkabah can take a multiplicity of forms. Sometimes they appear as a halo - an aura or envelope of light - associated with a master. Sometimes they occur as a column or pyramid of light. Often they are described as the spiritual body or the light body. The Merkabah is the body employed by a being in the fifth dimension in the same way that a physical body is employed by a being in the physical Universe, but at the same time it coordinates the overself with the human body. It is the embodiment of the higher self of each human being in the fifth dimension. The Merkabah is also an interdimensional craft that gives the ascended being unlimited freedom throughout the Universe. For this reason, in the Keys of Enoch, it is called the 'vehicle of vehicles'. The Merkabah vehicle is especially important for travel between the various dimensions of light because it can project itself from one life system or galaxy to the life system or galaxy of another universe by travelling in and out of physical space and time. It can do this because it has the ability to change the intrinsic speed of energy in every atom of its living fabric.

A Merkabah vehicle was the chariot of fire which carried away Elijah. A Merkabah vehicle was seen by Isaiah and witnessed by Ezekiel as 'wheels within wheels'. It was a Merkabah, hidden by a lenticular cloud, that carried Jesus Christ to heaven on his Ascension and it is a fleet of Merkabah vehicles that will lift humanity out of physical space and time in the three waves of ascension. The 'ships' of the Ashtar Command are not space-ships as we would imagine them to be. Terms such as 'ship' and 'command' are metaphors chosen for 20th Century communications just as 'chariots of fire' and 'winged angels' were used in bygone ages. These ships are living organisms, vast bio-technology systems. The largest, which can be as big as a small planet, are the "bio-satellites".

In the fifth dimension, biosatellites have been created to accommodate the population of the Earth whilst the Earth is cleansed prior to her ascension and the re-establishment of the biosphere on her surface. Biosatellites contain an internal atmosphere modified to suit its occupants, along with entire ecosystems and oceans, lakes and mountains and simulated night and day. They incorporate a sophisticated, living technology, far in advance of anything that even modern man can comprehend and they are not harsh and metallic but are organic, lush and verdant.

The Merkabah fleet manifests in the physical Universe in order to evacuate and accommodate individuals and plant and animal species during the col-

57

lapse of a planetary ecosystem. Millions of Merkabah vehicles are poised to descend and materialise in physical space and time, to evacuate the Earth at the time of the third wave of ascension. Physical evacuation will be offered to those wishing to avoid destruction, as the Earth enters the final phase of her transition into the ascended state.

Before this physical evacuation, those who are prepared to ascend will be beamed into the Merkabah by a teleportation process, described in the Keys of Enoch as transvirulance and in The Vortex: Key to Future Science as transubstantiation. Each individual will vanish out of physical space and time as they step into the opening of light at the end of a teleportation beam. On entering the beam they will be teleported into the 'heavenly' fifth dimension. Occurring in any one of three waves, the second aspect of the ascension will be the transmutation of the physical body into a fifth-dimensional, ascended body. It is this fifth-dimensional, light or diamond body that is ever youthful and subject to neither death nor disease; and each person who achieves this state, will also come into possession of a Merkabah vehicle, to accommodate them in the fifth dimension.

The Ashtar Command have predicted that those who ascend in the first wave will be given the opportunity to return to the Earth in the ascended state, to awaken the rest of humanity to the ascension opportunity. The Keys of Enoch support this prediction by speaking of the sudden appearance of 144,000 Ascended Masters on the Earth, who will transform the world and push back the clouds of darkness and de-

58

spair. The appearance of 144,000 masters is also predicted in the Native American prophecies as the "Rainbow Warriors" - a tribe from every colour and culture who would heal the Earth and bring humanity from the darkness into the light of true spiritual awareness. In April 1983, the Medicine Teacher, Harley Swiftdeer declared that "144,000 Sun Dance enlightened teachers will totally awaken in their dream mindbodies. They will begin to meet in their own feathered serpent or winged serpent wheels (Merkabah) and become a major force of light to help the rest of humanity to dance their dream awake..." This would also provide an explanation for the 144,000 spoken of in the Book of Revelation.

Chapter 7 of Revelation refers to an uncountable number from every nation clad in what John perceived to be white robes. This could have been his perception of the light bodies adorning the multitude, who follow in the wake of the 144,000 to rise in the second and third waves of ascension. John also said that these were the ones who had been cleansed by the time of great distress, a seven year period of great tribulation. This would correspond to the natural disasters that have been predicted as necessary in order for the Earth to cleanse herself of industrial civilisation and pollution prior to her own ascension. This is consistent with the ancient prophecy of St.Brigitte associated with St.Patrick. She had a vision in which she saw, as a result of Patrick's mission, a light spread throughout Ireland, and from Ireland throughout the world. But then in the last days, she saw the light go out in Ireland, and saw it return to a place of wild dogs and wild men. Then, seven years before the end, she saw Ireland disappear beneath the ocean. Many visionaries have seen southern England also inundated. (As a teenager, I was told by a psychic that within my lifetime London would be ninety foot under water.)

There are many warnings circulating throughout the world of massive Earth changes. These are supported by the ascension predictions. However, ascension is not intended as a preparation for disaster.

Ascension is the goal of all the self-transformation processing that human beings undertake in physical life on Earth. It corresponds to the final resurrection from death which is an integral part of the belief structure of a number of World religions. Ascension would appear to be available to anyone who acknowledges and respects the Creator - who can be known as love and life - and surrenders to this, which is their own innate reality.

The preparation for ascension could occur through any spiritual, religious or self-transformational practices or just by living a good life. The channelled information emphasises that it is less important what a person believes than how they live and practice true values. They also make it clear that no religious group has a monopoly on truth. This is certainly the basis of a more rational and scientific approach to 'spiritual matters', which are blighted by religious intolerance and sectarianism. If ascension is viewed as an evolutionary step it would seem obvious that personal qualitites rather than religious persuasions would establish the necessary criteria for this quantum leap. For this reason, all people are potential candidates for ascension but only those who have prepared themselves can take the leap.

For thousands of years religions have promised a spiritual life after death to those who subscribe to their exclusive ideologies. Science, as a reaction to religion, has denied all things spiritual and any form of survival after death. Science needs to be rescued from scepticism as religion needs to be rescued from sectarianism. Ascension is based more on science than religion. It is a bio-physical process which offers a means to live without the threat of death or the need to become enslaved to religion in order to enjoy universal freedom. We all need a way of truth and knowledge which will rescue us from bondage to the physical plane of existence and the endless round of birth and death, suffering, ageing and disease.

Ignoring fundamentalism in both science and religion, we can bring together the best elements of both these traditions and ascend to enjoy life without suffering death or disease in the higher dimensions of the Universe to which we already belong.

Chapter Five

The Ascension Plan

Sananda

Greetings my friends. I bring you a message which is important to all of mankind. My heart is full of love for each and every one of you. This is why I am here. I am the Good Shepherd. Some of you will know me in this modern time as Sananda, and others will know me as the one called Jesus the Christ.

The time for this planet and the people who inhabit her is running out. Do not be afraid because I bring a message of hope, not doom and gloom. This planet, when it was created by the Father God, my Father and your Father, was created in beauty and loveliness beyond compare and all the people and animals that dwelt therein lived in peace and harmony. Now, this wonderful Earth, so beloved by the Father God, has fallen into great decline and mankind will not listen. Very soon, my children, this planet will not be as you know her. The Earth will change as the all-loving God brings her back to the plan made in the first place. The world as you know it now - the climate, the famine, the disease, the pain, the torture, the hunger, the greed, the avarice - is coming to an end, and I have come through this instrument to tell you of a plan we have created for those of you who will listen and heed. We have called it the Ascension Plan.

The Ascension Plan is for you and for all the peoples of this Earth if they will but heed my word. The Godhead, the Father God, so loves this world that he sent me before to show you what could be accomplished if all men would live in peace and harmony. Yet those at that time sought to listen to only parts of my message and other parts were missed and have now been long forgotten, but this planet has still remained in the heart of the Father God, his most favoured, and her people upon the face of it, his most loved ones.

The Ascension Plan holds your salvation. It holds for you a place of safety. You need only to look at the newspapers and the reports of fires, floods and earthquakes to realise there is a great change coming upon the planet. Whilst loss of life cannot be avoided at this time, the Ascension Plan explains to you how you can overcome this. Thoughout the world there are thousands like yourselves who have come to hear the news of the Ascension. To many the news is greeted with something akin to remembrance that they have heard of this long before, but cannot place when. To others it is greeted with abhorrence and stupidity, mockery and cynicism. So be it, my children, I do not come to make people change their ways of life - their lifelong beliefs, their faith, their religion - I only come to tell them what is happening and how they may help themselves and others like them.

The Ascension Plan is divided into three main parts called the three waves of Ascension. The first wave of Ascension is already under way. Those already triggered into awakening by the Ascension message will be on this first wave of Ascension. They will be, for the most part, starseeds, that is people who have been programmed for Ascension even before they incarnated in this lifetime. The first wave we had anticipated would take somewhere in the region of 144,000 people.

The first wave will be a spiritual Ascension and will last from 2 - 48 hours. Those who have desired to go will be taken in spirit only: some in their sleep, others in a state of wakefulness, some in a state of meditation and others in a state where perhaps they remember nothing at all. On Ascension, you will be taken to a place which is prepared for you. You will know its love, you will feel its vibration, you will know the familiarity of the scenery, the place and the people therein. You need not be afraid, all that will surround you will be love and light and the wonderful Godhead Himself encompassing you with His love. Whilst you are there, there will be time for resting, there will be time for re-understanding, dusting down and generally making you feel a whole lot better. You will have come home.

The first wave is divided into two parts, those who desire to return to the Earthplane and those who don't. Each of you, whichever pathway you desire to take, will have the same knowledge of what will take place upon the Earthplane, and if you decide to return you will be returning as a different person. You will be connecting with your Higher-self so that you can bring back into this bodily form and your environment in which you live, the spiritual essence and some of the things you are capable of but perhaps, as yet, have remained dormant. Those of you who are healers will find that your healing abilities will have been enhanced many times. You will find that the healing that you give will be almost instantaneous. Those of you who are willing to channel information on the Ascension will find many facets of myself available to you - only ask in love and you shall receive.

There will be other things as well that will be enhanced within you. You may notice a difference in your bodily form. Your bodies will cease to age and decay in physiological terms, they will begin to regress to their prime. Young people will continue to grow to their prime. The starseeds who return back to their environment and families, and mundane world, will be ready to assist those who are asking questions. They will be ready to assist groups and explain to them what is happening - to show them, prepare them, ease the way for them and calm their fears so when the second wave begins, they will be ready.

So to the second wave. I cannot give you dates as it is not permitted and I would not like to evoke mass panic on the planet Earth (it will be in a time of years rather than centuries) but the second wave is the beginning of the evacuation. The changes that will occur on this planet will be so great and so cataclysmic that it would not be right for any of you to be on her surface when this occurs. This is what the Ascension Plan is designed for. It is a plan of awareness, heightened sensitivity and temporary evacuation.

After the first wave, many will have returned to spread the news of the Ascension Plan. We are hoping that this will make things easier for people to leave this Earth for a while because the second and third waves must be the Ascension of the body and the spirit. Those of you who choose to do that, you will

66

afford great assistance to the many who remain here before the final evacuation.

The final wave will be the last chance for Ascension. Those who choose to remain behind will miss their chance and will go through the death process. Some will be taken to another place where their souls will be restructured. Some may even return to the dimensions or the other worlds from which they have come because there are other worlds - you are not the only ones in this vast Universe. The Universes that even you do not know of are innumerable. I could not begin to count them, and within these Universes are planets with beings of light, beings of physical shape much like your own, and beings who just exist in thought and light alone, but beings they are.

So some of those will return to the dimensions from whence they came and others will be helped along their way and their pain made bearable, but any at that final wave who express the desire to be with the Father God then, so be it, we will take them. No one is barred.

The final days will come as soon as the evacuation of the third wave has been completed. The Earth will shift on her axis. She will change - north may become south and south become north and what was wet may become dry and what was dry may become wet. You may see the sun rise in the west and set in the east. There will be a change in the climate and there will be a shuddering and breaking of the Earth's surface. The Earth will be reshaped to my Father's original design. This is truth. This is no story - it is happening now. There will be more flooding, there will be more shaking of the Earth, there will be more fire, and also the destruction of wealth. The trappings which many people think they must have here will be destroyed and in their place they will learn that these things are not important.

As I have said, it is not doom and gloom and it is not going to happen next week. Watch and look around to see what is happening. Understand and with that understanding in your hearts tell those who are still ignorant of what is happening. When the final wave has been completed you may do as you please, you may stay in the created environment or you may return to the new Earth - you may walk between the two.

Your bodily form will be changed, your spiritual will undoubtedly be changed. You will have no need of the vehicles which run on your roads, and again, turn to your western Bible, the lion will lay down with the lamb. You are on the brink of a new dawn for all mankind. Some call it the 'New Age'. Some call it the 'Age of Aquarius'. We call it the birth of the world. It is an exciting and wonderful age in which you live and each and every one of you, your families, your fathers, your husbands, your wives, your daughters, your sons - each and every one of you has the opportunity to return and see this world as it should have been and as it will be!

You will walk upon the face of the Earth again. Do not think for one moment that in the third and final phase, that is it. Nay, you will return. You will return to see your grandchildren grow but in such a world that only your wildest dreams and imaginings you have seen. This is no fantasy, this is no story, this is happening now - your world is changing. With the love that is in my heart and with the love that I bring from the Father God, will you not heed my words? Will you not look, will you not listen? Tell your friends and help them to understand!

Man has progressed; perhaps too much progression. Man has been given the technology and yet he uses it to destroy his world rather than assist. Man has abused the greatest gift of all which is the world in which he lives. Technology is always being updated and heightened and yet he fails to eradicate the disease which is responsible for killing more human beings than anything else on this Earthplane and that disease is greed. That is why half this planet starves and the other half is at war - you have no idea how much this grieves me. This is why I am here, this is why I have chosen to speak to all who will hear me again. This is not a new message, neither is it a new Sermon on the Mount - it is a plan for your continued race, without it you will surely perish. My Father, the Godhead, will see that no hair on your heads is harmed, this is why He offers to you so freely the Ascension Plan.

I would like to leave you with a meditation which is especially designed to help you reach higher. You may use it at any time. First of all I would like you to understand there are various points on the spiritual body which act as openings to spiritual attainment. You have a name for them which is chakras.

When you are relaxed I want you to take in two or three gentle breaths and focus on the rhythm of your breathing, gently in and gently out. Now I want you to imagine above you a beautiful beam of white light and as you open your chakra centres I want you to take the beam of light through the top of your head and bring it right through the whole of your body, spreading to your toes, the tip of your nose, your ears, everything about you. Let this wonderful white light penetrate everything. As you are sitting in it's warmth I want you to allow it to penetrate further. I want you to let it filter through your bones, through to the inner organs. Illuminate them, getting rid of any undesirable things there, any pain. Cover it in white light, every corner, and still further filter this through to your blood, the little corpuscles running around your body at this time, every one of them little pinpoints of light. Feel the energy coursing through you.

Now I want you to imagine yourselves in a cool quiet place of your choice. You may choose a temple, a pyramid or a favourite room; somewhere confined where you may sit and illuminate yourself with this light. Now I want you to imagine a doorway out. I want you to gently rise, turn towards the doorway and walk through. It is light, it is warm, your feet touch the green grass. There is beauty and peace all around you. The air is heavy with birdsong and in the distance you can hear the gentle tinkle of a stream. The sunshine is bright and covers you in warmth and love like the arm of the Father God.

Walk towards this stream, see the clarity of the water, and yet it is not cold, it is warm to the touch. Bathe yourself in it's healing waters, let it carry away in it's path the dross and dullness of this world. Let it take away your pain, your heartbreak, all things that will tie you to this Earth - let them float gently away.

As you step out on the other side you are invigorated, strangely at peace and shining bright. Look towards the front and can you see a mountaintop that reaches high into the clear air? Isn't that the place you would like to be; atop the mountain where you can clearly see everything? Then go for that mountaintop, not with your feet but with your thoughts. If you want to go beyond the mountaintop it is well within your reach.

Go through the skies to touch the stars, look back on your world, bright and shining in the sky. It is your world, you have created it thus, you have healed it. Gently return to the mountaintop, feel it's coolness. Take it deep within you; the serenity and peace. Come once more to the riverbank, find yourself within the doorway, come in. Freely partake of the ambience of warmth around you and return here with us.

Move your fingers and toes, wriggle your toes and know that you are firmly planted here. Sad though it may be I am afraid that you have to stay here for a while. Now it is important that you listen to what I say. Once you have finished this meditation or any others it is important you close your chakra centres. You can imagine them as you like, little portholes, windows, doors, but you must seal them, seal the energy and light, serenity and peace in. Close each of them individually and seal it with love. Do this each time you wish to partake of this meditation or any other occasion when you open your chakras in this way.

Now my loved ones, my time here for the moment is finished. My parting words to you are only to think on what I have said. Think them over, think them through and question within yourselves. Try and find others who are of like mind to yourselves. Speak of this change. Watch the changing face of the Earth and know that Sananda has told you the truth. The Ascension Plan is for all of you. Be happy in this and know that if you have the simplicity of love in your hearts, the desire to help your fellow men, and above all the desire to be part of the change in this world - each and everyone of you shall partake in the Ascension - none shall be barred. Hear this my children, none shall be barred: no race, no colour, no religion, no Jew, no gentile.

This shall pass away and in it's place will be a union of all mankind, and with that union of mankind will come the union of life itself, and with the union of life itself the union of the Father God and His children is inevitable. This is what the Ascension can do for you. The Ascension is given freely and I ask only that you accept it in love and you take it freely. Therefore, my loved ones, as the Father freely gives to you, freely receive, freely partake and freely share. Unify your causes, work together in peace and harmony. Let none think he is better than the other for in the sight of the Father God, all are equal. There are others who will help you, there are others who know and understand. For now I leave you my love and the love from your Father God. Know that it is He who watches and it is He who waits. May love and light remain always in your lives and I hope, until we meet again, that love be your goal. Farewell my friends.

Channelled through the Amethyst Group
Dawlish, Devon, EX7 0QX, U.K.
January - March,1994

Chapter Six

Ascension & the Soul

"Ascension is the process whereby the soul, having balanced its karma and fulfilled its divine plan, merges first with the Christ Consciousness and then with the life presence of the I AM THAT I AM. Once the ascension has taken place, the soul, the non-permanent aspect of being, becomes the incorruptible core, a permanent atom in the Body of God"

St. Germaine

I teach that the soul consists of the three higher bodies of man, beyond the physical body. These three bodies belong to the hyper-physical levels of the Universe, or the lower-creation worlds.

The lowest body of the soul is the morphic or etheric field which controls the morphogenesis or differentiation of the physical body. This body governs the health and well-being of the physical body. The energy in this body is called 'chi' by the Chinese and 'prana' by the Indians. Wilhelm Reich described it as orgone energy. All living organisms have morphic fields, which are apparent in Kirlian photographs.

The second level of the soul is the astral or emotional body. Animals have astral bodies as well as morphic fields.

The third and highest level of the soul is the psychic or mental body. Human beings have morphic, astral and psychic bodies. The soul is merely a higher level of body. It is the embodiment of consciousness in the hyper-physical realms of the Universe, as the physical body is the embodiment of consciousness in the physical realms.

If you imagine the physical body as a space-suit we don in order to live on a physical planet, the soul could be imagined as undergarments. Neither the body nor the soul are permanent or immortal. They have the potential to become immortal. At death, the spirit discards first the body and then the soul. For each incarnation it enters a new soul and a new body. The spirit self creates fresh souls, much like the individuals in a species. Each soul has different experiences and learns new lessons in each incarnation. In this way karma is balanced for the spirit self.

Ascension is the process whereby the final soul and body in a chain of incarnations become immortalised so that the spirit self can re-enter the hyper-physical and physical realms of the Universe without having to enter a cycle of incarnations and go through the birth and death process. If a being fails to make the ascension at the end of a cycle of incarnations, it enters a new cycle.

One could imagine a cycle of incarnations as a term at school. At the end of term there is an examination. Life in the 20th.Century is the examination. There is something here to distract every soul from the call of the spirit to ascension. Materialism or religious fundamentalism, people, places and things all attract souls which are not yet ready to ascend. Only those who can resist the temptations and devote themselves to the spirit of truth, selfless service and unconditional love, will be ready and prepared to respond to the call to ascend, which will occur suddenly and without warning - that is part of the test.

Ascension is the graduation from school. For those who graduate with honours there is the opportunity of the equivalent of 'a place at University or a good job' in the higher realms of the Universe. For those who fail the examination, it is back to school for another term of lessons. In the year 2012 the planet Earth is ascending. She is being upgraded from school to university, and will be available to ascension graduates only. Schooling will continue on other planets elsewhere in the physical planes of the Universe. This is the fulfilment of the prediction by Christ that "the meek shall inherit the Earth" because the curriculum of the planetary school is love. We are being tested, not on our powers, abilities or physical achievements, but on our ability to love one another unconditionally.

Immortality for the body and the soul is the diploma each being receives on ascension, along with the freedom of the Universe and eternal life.

Many people ask why it is necessary for the physical body to be immortalised. The same question could be asked of the soul. The soul is just a higher level of body or 'vehicle' for the spirit. In the ascension all levels of body or 'vehicle' are lifted and immortalised so that the spirit has a permanent vehicle for entering the lower levels of the Universe.

The spirit consists of nine embodiments of consciousness in the super-physical levels of the Universe, which are divided into the mid- and high-creation worlds. The mid-creation worlds extend from the fifth level to the ninth level and the high-creation worlds extend from the tenth to the thirteenth levels. Levels ten and eleven are also realms of the group self.

Within the mid-creation worlds, levels five to seven (the seventh heaven) are the realms of the higher self and levels eight and nine are the realms of the group self. These are the levels wherein the spirit merges with the Christ Consciousness.

Within the high-creation worlds, levels ten and eleven are realms of the group-self. Levels twelve and thirteen are the realms of the one-self; the state of being at one with all that is. These are the levels wherein the spirit merges with the life presence of the I AM.

> *But love, endless love,*
> *In a flood that knows no bounds,*
> *Will gush forth from the soul,*
> *And will sweep the world around,*
> *If the soul is only open ...*

Chapter Seven

The Starseeds

There are two directions in which consciousness is evolving through the Universe. The first direction involves the descent of conscious life from the highest to the lowest levels of the Universe. The second direction involves the ascent of conscious life from the lowest to the highest.

The Higher Bodies of Man

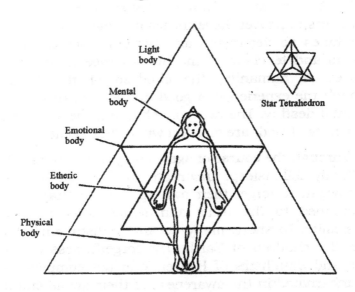

Light body

Mental body

Emotional body

Etheric body

Physical body

Star Tetrahedron

The first direction could be described as the 'Children of Heaven'. By the Ascended Masters they are often described as 'The Descended Masters.' These are the sons and daughters of God by birth. They are spiritual beings that come into being in the high- and mid-creation worlds and have descended to the low-creation worlds to experience physicality and in some cases to support the 'Children of Earth' in their evolution and awakening from physicality into spirituality.

Through the process of ascension, the children of the Earth become the sons and daughters of God by adoption. This is the second direction of spiritual evolution.

In the course of human history the sons and daughters of heaven have incarnated again and again sometimes as destroyers and tyrants, sometimes as healers and teachers of the human race to lead the masses of humanity, the children of the Earth, through the experience of good and evil, toward their spiritual destiny. The heavenly children, the sons and daughters of God, are also known as 'Starseeds'.

Through the course of ages, many of the starseeds gradually fell asleep. Incarnate in physical bodies, they began to forget their own spiritual heritage and succumbed to the trials and temptations of their physicality. In short, many became indistinguishable from the children of Earth. The forgetfulness of the sons and daughters of Heaven was not complete. A few incarnated in the awareness of their divine status and walked the earth as enlightened leaders and spiritual teachers. At the same time many children of Earth, under the stimulation of these teachers, awakened to their spiritual destiny and became saints or sages in their own right. The result of this process through the ages, has been a levelling of the children of Heaven and the children of Earth so that as we approach the ascension, all stand equal before God, as fragments of the one Divine Being.

Sin means 'separation from source'. The children of Heaven took on the veil of illusion - or the original sin of separation from their higher spirit selves - in order to join the cycles of physical incarnations. In this way they voluntarily came down to the level of physicality, forgetfulness and limitation. They took on the burden of suffering of the children of Earth to set an example of how it is possible to overcome sin or separation from source through a life of selfless service and unconditional love. These saints of the long ages of man have, by their example, helped the children of Earth to evolve from physical to spiritual beings.

In times of great difficulty and darkness, Beings from the highest level of the Godhead, will step down into the 'frequency of physicality', and incarnate without the veil of separation from source or forgetfulness of previous lives on Earth. These 'Immaculate Conceptions' or 'Avatars' live and work in the full knowledge of their Divinity and power to awaken the Earthlings and sleepy Starseeds.

"I have been born many times, Arjuna, and many times have you been born. But I remember my past lives, and you have forgotten yours.

"Although I am unborn, everlasting, and I AM the Lord of all, I come to my realm of nature and through my wonderous power I AM born.

"When righteousness is weak and faints and unrighteousness exults in pride, then my Spirit arises on Earth

"For the salvation of those who are good, for the destruction of evil in men, for the fulfilment of the kingdom of righteousness, I come into this world in the ages that pass.

"He who knows my birth as God and who knows my sacrifice, when he leaves his mortal body, goes no more from death to death, for he in truth comes to me."

(Bhagavad Gita: 4:5-9)

For unto us a child is born, unto us a son is given: and the government shall be upon his shoulder: and his name shall be called Wonderful Counseller, The Mighty God, the everlasting Father, the Prince of Peace.

(Isaiah 9:6)

The problem with these Immaculate of Divine incarnations was that they stood apart from humanity and came to be worshipped as God. Divine incarnations have occurred as much to teach God about man as man about God. Establishing cults around Divine incarnations, humankind have denied the growth of their own innate divinity or divine potential. Avatars came to show us the way to realise God within ourselves, not to be worshipped as God in the external.

"The Kingdom of God comes not with observation: neither shall they say, 'Lo here! or lo there!' for behold, the Kingdom of God is within you."

(Luke Chapter 17:20-21)

Because of the danger of idolatry - that is the worship of an extrnalised God - even at the starseed level, it has been necessary for Starseeds to forget their divine status and work amongst the children of Earth as Earthlings. At the moment of ascension, however, there will be no difference between the children of Heaven and children of Earth. Though their origins may be different, each will have been through the same trials and tribulations of terrestrial life to test their spiritual worth and their ability to love unconditionally and apply themselves to spiritual service.

It is the prerogative of the Creator to create some children through physical, chemical and biological evolution, and others through direct spiritual manifestation. On ascension each child of God comes into their light body of Cosmic Christ Consciousness. For the children of Heaven it is an awakening to what they have forgotten: for the children of Earth it is an awakening to what they have forged.

Starseeds and Earthlings ascend as equals. Each child of God will come to spiritual maturity through passing through the same baptism of suffering in this world of limitation. Each will have learned the same lessons in this terrestrial school. Each creature will come before the Creator with the wisdom of spirit that

81

only suffering and endurance through difficulty, challenge and adversity can bring.

Just as the higher and lower selves find their integration in the human heart, so the children of Heaven and the children of Earth complete their integration and come into divine adulthood on their ascension. The children of Heaven knew paradise only with the innocence of children. There was no appreciation because there was no contrasting experience. As the children of Heaven relinquished paradise in order that the children of Earth might come to enjoy it too, they allowed themselves the contrasting experience to enable them to appreciate Heaven. Leaving home, the children went out into the wilderness to collect their orphan kin. Older and wiser, they will all return after endless trials and difficulties. Imagine their joy! For some it is the long-awaited return home: for others it is a new and fresh experience. For all it is Heaven after Hell; the ultimate experience in appreciation. No longer as children in the home, by virtue of birth and parental obligation, we would be in our heavenly home as young adults, full of experiences, wisdom and maturity. This is the purpose of the descent and ascent of humankind. There is no shame in sin or separation. There is nothing to fear. We are all like the prodigal son spoken of by Jesus (Luke 15:11-32).

The son left home and separated from the father in order to explore the world, seek his fortune and gain experience. In the end the son lost everything. Only in his misfortune did he long once more for home. When he returned home he imagined he would be rejected for his loss. Instead he was welcomed by his father with joy and feasting. The one that was lost was found. He that was separated from the father was returned.

So it is with us all. We separated out from the source as offshoots of the Divine. We descended through the many levels of the Universe and have come away so far from Source that not only have we forgotten that in our essence we are God, we have begun to doubt the very existence of God. Whilst things go well for us we wander further from our spiritual home. Fascinated by things in the material world, we have a good time and enjoy ourselves and our spiritual home is far from our minds. However, as things begin to go wrong in our lives - perhaps misfortune or disease strikes us down - we begin to question the meaning and purpose of our lives. We begin to long for our spiritual home.

Like the prodigal son, we have to be reduced to rags before we turn our attention from physical distractions to our spiritual purpose.

Many people wonder why a loving God allows suffering and pain in the world. Spirits grow wise through suffering. Through suffering they learn compassion and lose their pride. A degree of suffering is an essential part of spiritual and human evolution.

As many as I love, I rebuke and chasten...

(Revelation 3:19)

83

It is said "No pain no gain". We need to experience pleasure but this has to be balanced with pain. In the words of Lord Krishna to Arjuna:

"From the world of the senses, Arjuna, comes heat and comes cold, and pleasure and pain. They come and they go: they are transient. Arise above them strong soul.

"The man whom these cannot move, whose soul is one, beyond pleasure and pain, is worthy of life in Eternity. "

(Bhagavad Gita 2:14-15)

The karmic balancing of pain and pleasure, in our many incarnations prior to ascension, has nothing to do with punishment and reward. It merely provides us all with a balance of experience through which we can evolve and grow as spiritual beings. The Earth could go through great changes prior to her ascension. This would involve unavoidable pain and suffering. Many people fear the predicted Earth changes, but the wise ones see that they could be a necessary part of the process of human ascension. They may be the only way to divert humanity from materialism to spirituality, from going ever further out from spirit into material. The time has come for us to go home. If the material illusion has to be swept away in order that we let go of it, then it will be swept away.

Three waves of ascension have been predicted and it is likely that each wave of ascension will coincide with a wave of Earth changes. If the great Earth changes come, see them not as a disaster but as a sign of deliverance. Understand the loving parent who has to take away our playthings when the time comes for us to leave the playground and return home.

This world is only a playground. Forgetting the inner child, we have forgotten that physical life is but play to spirit. Losing touch with our spiritual nature we have come to take the physical world too seriously.

"Unless you accept the Kingdom of Heaven as a little child you shall not enter it".

(Luke 18:17)

We need to discover the inner child and realise that we are only children of God who have come into the world to learn and grow and play. We have nothing to fear of our parents. The Father/Mother deities are not punishing us by taking away our toys. They take away the terrestrial playground from humankind only so that they will return home for rest and re-creation.

There is another day to look forward to - new games and adventures in the Universal playground in new cycles of evolution. We have to let go of the old in order to accept the new. Our clothes have to be reduced to rags and our worldly treasures have to be taken away. Only then will we let go of them and allow our heavenly parents to adorn us in the raiment of the light body and heap upon us the treasure of the gods.

The plan of ages slowly unfolds,
Within its great purpose man evolves,
Ages of suffering grim to bear,
But how else would we learn,
To love care and share...

85

Chapter Eight

Ascension &
Christians

Ascension is the fulfilment of the predictions for the coming New Age of enlightenment and peace. It is the rapture expected by the Christians. Unfortunately it has become common practice for some people, who call themselves Christian, to condemn the New Age Movement as the work of the devil and treat people in the New Age movement as servants of Satan. Sadly, the ascension movement is included in their wholesale damnation of anything that does not come directly from the Bible.

In the Bible Jesus warned us not to judge others.

"Do not judge others, or you will be judged. For in the same way as you judge others, you will be judged and with the measure you use, it will be measured to you.

"Why do you look at the speck of sawdust in your brother's eye and pay no attention to the plank in your own eye.

"You hypocrite, first take the plank out of your own eye, then you can see clearly to remove the speck from your brother's eye."

(Matthew 7:1-5.)

In the action of damning others we damn ourselves. If we call others servants of Satan, we declare
ourselves as such, because as we judge others, so we
will be judged. In the Bible Jesus Christ commanded
us to love one another. If we are true Christians we
will be known by our love, not by our condemnation
of others. Reasons to condemn people in the New Age
movement can be found in the Bible, but then for
centuries false Christians have found reasons in the
Bible to hate and persecute others who do not share
their beliefs because the Bible can be used to justify
anything including murder and infanticide!

"Happy is he who dashes your infants against the
rocks."

(Psalm 137:9)

True Christians only use the Bible to inspire them
in their love. True Christians love unconditionally,
recognising the "Christ" in everyone regardless of their
race, colour or creed.

All religious and spiritual groups, be they Christian or New Age contain hipocrites, but they also
contain sincere seekers after truth. The New Age 'ascension' movement is full of true Christians. They ra-
diate joy and gentleness. They are devoted to serving
humanity and beloved Earth. You will know them by
their love. They are open to the Bible and to channellings, but then the Bible is full of channelling. Channelling is just a new word for prophecy. The Bible is a
record of channellings of spirit or prophecy, that occurred thousands of years ago. Even the Gospels of
Jesus were channelled. They were inspired re-

cordings of the life and teachings of Jesus, written decades after his ascension.

The Bible warned us that there would be an increase in prophecy in the last days. Whilst exercising discernment of the spirit, a true Christian will be as open to the word of God in this day as in any day that has gone before.

In the beginning was the word and the word was with God and the word was God

(John 1:1)

And the Word became flesh and dwelt amongst us.

(John 1:14)

Jesus Christ is revealed in the Bible as the living word of God which became flesh and dwelt amongst us. True Christians live according to the teachings of Jesus Christ whom they believe to be resurrected and alive with us today. It should come as no surprise to us to hear Jesus speak to us, in our present day and age, through a modern channel or prophet. In fact we should be awaiting his call because in the Bible we have been told to expect that in the last days, the Elect will be called. The call for ascension could be the long-awaited call for the Elect.

All Christians believe they are amongst the Elect, but only those who are open to new prophecy will be open to the call when it comes. Christians who reject anything that is not in the Bible exclude themselves from the Elect because they are closed to all post-Biblical calls from God. The Elect are the true and faithful servants of God who are open to the call of spirit in the end and most testing times of human history.

We all have demonic as well as angelic spirit guides. Christians condemn the New Age Movement because it opens people up to guidance from spirit without discrimination between angelic and demonic inspirations. The test for us all is to exercise discernment in every sphere of our lives. When dealing with channelled information we have to be very discerning because it all contains a mix of truth and falsehood. We have to judge in our hearts what we feel to be true or false. The truth will cause us to feel joy and upliftment while falsehoods will cause us to feel irritated or depressed. The adventure of life is to follow our joy through ascension into eternal life.

We need to heed the warnings of Jesus Christ given in the Bible. He warned us to pray and be ever vigilant to prepare for the day of ascension or rapture, which will be known to no one until it arrives:

"But of that day and that hour, no man knows, nor the angels in heaven, neither the Son, but the Father.

"Take heed, watch and pray: for you not know when the time is.

"For the Son of Man is like a man who took a far journey. He left his house and gave authority to his servants, and to every man his work, and commanded the porter to watch.

"Watch therefore: for you know not when the master of the house comes, at evening, midnight or at the cockcrowing, or in the morning: lest coming suddenly he find you sleeping.

*"And what I say to you I say to all, **keep watch**."*

(Mark 13:32-37)

Chapter Nine

Ascension & Evolution

The soul can ascend into the fifth dimension after the death process. At the time of the third wave of ascension it is predicted that billions of souls will be ascending from the fourth dimension into the fifth. Physical ascension is not essential to immortalise the soul. However, physical ascension is important for the preservation of DNA.

Physical ascension could to occur at any time in order to save DNA in the face of a mass extinction of species. This represents the *Omega Point* of an evolutionary cycle of that species.

It is well documented that mass extinctions of species have occurred on the Earth in it's history. Mass extinction of the human species could occur through nuclear war, ecological collapse, a shift of the Earth on her axis, a comet or asteroid strike or a burst of solar radiation, scorching the Earth by fire. The physical ascension of humans, prior to an extinction process, would allow for a continuity of humans on Earth, if they are returned after the cataclysm has occurred and the Earth re-stabilised.

It is not necessary to ascend every member of a species in order to save the DNA. As occurred, at the time of Noah and the Deluge, samples of species were saved, along with a human family to re-establish breeding populations after the extinction event wiped out most creatures alive on Earth. The story of the flood serves to tell that the salvage of a relatively small sample would be sufficient to ensure the continuity of the species. Through the ascension process species, or specific members of a particular species could be selectively salvaged according to criteria established by the beings operating the process. Whatever, or whoever is left behind would die in the mass extinction. Ascension and extinction could be seen as a natural selection process in the evolution of the Universe. The Ashtar Command could be seen as the ET version of Noah's Ark.

Mass extinction, representing the end of a cycle of evolution, offers an opportunity of cleansing the planet of parasites and disease organisms which accumulate in the evolutionary process.

Parasites are early biological models that have not been successful on the 'open range'. They escaped the execution of extinction by preying on more successful species. For example, the earliest worms were a tube with a single muscle wall. However, when they moved toward lunch, by a wave of contraction passing down the muscles, this peristalsis expelled breakfast out of the tube. It was impossible for these early worms to move and digest and assimilate their food. The problem was overcome by putting a split in the wall of muscle so that the waves of contraction enabling the worm to move were separated from the peristalsis involved in their feeding.

Earthworms are an example of these successful Mark II model worms. In fact, we have evolved from this improvement and have our locomotive muscles separated from our alimentary canal muscles.

The Mark I model worms, unable to eat and move have found a place where they can eat without moving. They inhabit other creatures as parasites. These are the nematode worms which plague every other species on Earth. Tape worms, pin worms, flukes and round worms are included in their numbers. These creatures should surrender to extinction. Instead they cause disease and suffering throughout the biosphere as a result of their inherent deficiencies.

A parasite is an organism which cares only for itself, taking from another creature without care for its welfare. It is essentially selfish in its behaviour. All creatures must have an element of selfishness in order to survive. Predators serve the prey by culling out weak, old, diseased members of the prey species thus protecting the prey herd from epidemics and over-population. They serve the survival of the fittest. Parasites cause disease. They bring down strong members of their host species. The parasite takes selfishness to the extreme by destroying the host. It does not benefit the host species but moves onto another unfortunate victim to ensure its survival.

It is clearly apparent that many humans are exhibiting parasitic traits. They have become planetary parasites as a result of their spiritual insufficiencies. Selective ascension ensures that only those who do not exhibit parasitic traits will escape extinction when all parasites are extinguished with the completion of the present phase of evolution on Earth

Humans have become the equivalent to parasites on the Earth. Plundering the host planet for resources and polluting their home, Homo Sapiens is looking toward the stars for new planets to colonise as the Earth dies beneath it's feet, much as a parasite looks for a new host to invade as it kills the host it is on. It is only to be expected that the Universe should seek to protect itself from us as we begin to develop the technology for space travel before anti-gravity free energy craft enable us to escape the Earth. The preservation of caring and loving human beings, through ascension, to safeguard the species, whilst allowing those who behave as planetary pathogens to become extinct - in the cleansing of the Earth - would appear to make sense in an intelligent Universe.

Whether we believe in the ascension or not isn't the issue. We may scoff at the idea that all humans on Earth today are being monitored by highly advanced extra-terrestrial beings who have teleportation technologies all lined up for ascension. We may object to the idea that they are making selections from the simple, day-by-day arts of care and kindness, compassion and unconditional love that individuals exhibit toward other people, other species and the planet itself. However, we cannot deny that we are heading for disaster, be it nuclear, ecological or astronomical. Ecologically, we are confronted with extinction within fifty years unless the present onslaught on the environment is arrested. There is no sign of the brakes being applied rather the accelerator is hitting the floor!

We have no way of knowing if we will be saved until the moment of ascension is upon us, just as we will have no way of knowing if we are to be extinguished until extinction is imminent, so it is worth living our lives out of unconditional love to optimise our survival, spiritually and physically.

Our lives and the lives of others will be better for our acts of care and kindness whilst we live, so we have nothing to lose by living for ascension. If the ascension message is true, even if we don't believe in it, by our love we will qualify for it and we may be in for a pleasant surprise. Every human being has the opportunity to ascend. We each have choices in our attitudes and behaviour on a moment-to-moment basis. Everyone has the opportunity to be unselfish, to act in courage out of love and care for others and the whole. The ascension is a form of natural selection, but for us it is more a 'self-selection' process.

There is one life in the many organisms. Just as life does not expect all acorns to make oak trees, so life does not expect everyone to make it through to ascension. Life is evolving. It supports quantity in order to maximise the opportunity of achieving top quality in those who survive the selection process.

LOVE IN ACTION

It is up to you to decide if you want to be the seed of mortality that grows into the tree of immortality. All you have to do is seek opportunities to act out of love and kindness and care as you go about your daily life. Seek opportunities to serve the Spirit of Truth in yourself and in others. Allow joy and laughter to be expressed in your being. Let go of your attachment to people, places and things. Constantly witness yourself - in your thoughts, words and deeds - and seek opportunities to heal and be healed in body, mind and spirit. Let go of addictions and compulsive patterns of behaviour. Take every opportunity to exercise conscious choice in your thinking and doing. Come into your power as a self-conscious, self-determining being. Become a master of yourself *now*, so that you are prepared to be a master in the ascended state. Come into command of yourself now because as a 'commander' it will be you and you alone who you will command.

Breathe consciously as you go about your daily life. Allow your breath to go slow and deep so that you feel into the centre of well being and fulfilment in the heart. We each have to get out of the head and get into the heart. Conscious breathing and acts of selfless service and unconditional love will bring you into the ascension moment by moment, day by day. Gently surrendering attachment to relationships and possessions, relinquishing judgements, jealous criticism and rigid beliefs, letting go of incarcerating attitudes, trivial pre-occupations and addictions, is the process that enables you to move from mortality to immortality and the freedom of the Universe.

Your love is expressed in your works. It is no good saying you care but not acting out of your compassion. There are so many things we can all be doing to help and inspire others. It is all too easy to sit in judgement of others whilst sitting in preoccupation with our own self-interests. The Universe is looking for people who demonstrate love in action. It seeks people who walk their talk. There is so much to be done. We can show our love for the Earth by planting trees and clearing trash. We can exercise our compassion by sharing our time with lonely people instead of the television. Never in human history has there been such a need coupled with an opportunity to serve. Whatever you can do, do it now because your time on Earth is limited!

Though we may love the Earth we are not here forever. Many people say they don't want to ascend because they don't want to leave the Earth. What they do not seem to appreciate is that, notwithstanding reincarnation, it is only people who have ascended that are able to stay with the Earth for more than a few decades. Most people leave the Earth well within a hundred years. Ascended Masters such as Baba Ji and St.Germaine have been with the Earth for centuries. The Blessed Mother Mary has been appearing regularly for two thousand years and Thoth has been around for fifty thousand years. So if you want to stay with the Earth go for the ascension before death tears you away.

We are not here to become attached to the Earth. We are here to learn our lessons, evolve and move on into the immensity of the Universe as responsible galactic citizens and planetary guardians. We have all become too attached to this world when there are billions of others to explore and cultivate. But with freedom of the Universe comes responsibility. Non-interference and respect for other life-forms, cultures and peaceful civilisations is expected of star travellers, and the human track record in this respect is not good. We have to prove to the Universe our ability to love and care and respect before we are to be given freedom to roam the galaxies.

Many people demand *Proof for Truth* before they will believe anything. I tell you, at this time each and every individual is being called upon to prove their truth. 20th Century civilisation is a test set to establish how true each and every human being really is. Those who prove true will ascend into immortality and eternal life. Those who prove false face extinction. The Universe is not sentimental. We are living organisms so we all participate in the evolutionary process of which natural selection is an essential part. Organisms that don't make the grade perish and the grade for us all is love. Who we are and what we believe is unimportant. It matters how we live and how we love. But more than anything it is how we live out our love that counts.

ENERGY AND CONSCIOUSNESS

The thing about us that is real is our conscious awareness. This is the I AM presence within us. This is the divinity which we embody. This is the aspect of God in a mammalian body which we each are. All else is illusion, so this is the time of disillusionment. We have to become disillusioned with the illusion. That is what disappointment achieves.

The Universe of energy - with all of its levels and dimensions - is insubstantial. It is just the dream of God, the Universal Intelligence which brings everything into existence, particle by particle, as conscious acts of abstraction. Everything outside of our conscious awareness is not it, is not real, is the Universal illusion.

It is what we do with our attention that counts. If our attention is always focused on thoughts and emotions and the body, its well-being, appearance, comfort and survival, then we trap consciousness in the physical and hyper-physical realms of the Universe. We keep divinity locked in illusion.

If, however, we bring our attention into the breath this diverts the focus of consciousness into the heart centre which is the doorway to ascension. This is the opening to the fifth dimension, the link to the merkabah, the gateway out of the hyper-physical and into the super-physical. This leads us into the spiritual regions of the Universe where the ascended ones dwell.

So evolve and ascend, as is your life-right and remember that surrender is acceptance of what is happening in your life. You are being perfectly prepared for ascension now. Just let the perfect process unfold in your life. Accept and allow. Breathe consciously and laugh - laugh and find your joy. Be who you truly are, the crown of creation, and ascend into your glory.

Having learnt the lessons of love and completed its mission on Earth to gain wisdom through knowledge of good and evil in the realms of limitation, the lower self has the opportunity, through ascension, to merge with the higher self. Thus complete, the human being has the potential for unlimited joy, growth, freedom and evolution in the ever expanding Universe

ENERGY AND THE FALL

I believe that the speed of energy is not uniform throughout the Universe. I believe that the general speed of energy in the Universe could be a lot faster than the speed of common light. I am of the opinion that the speed of energy in and around the Earth is depressed because it is presently located in what I describe as a Zone of Density.

Within this zone the speed of energy has dropped to the speed of light, so that light from distant stars appears to be travelling at 186,000 miles per second when, in fact, as it left it's original source it could have been travelling very much faster. For example, according to Ashtar, the star system of Arcturus is fifth-dimensional, so light from that system would travel faster than the light in our world. However, on entering the zone of density in which we are located, it would drop in speed to that of physical light, so that that Arcturus would appear to be a third dimensional star system.

I believe that we have been in a three dimensional zone of density for tens if not hundreds of thousands of years. The purpose has been to contain us in quarantine whilst we learnt important lessons on how to rise above selfishness and greed and live in love. The Earth has not always been in this zone of density. It's arrival here corresponded to the 'Fall' - a literal fall in the intrinsic speed of energy in every atom that forms it. The ascension is the reversal of the Fall. It is a return of the speed of energy in the Earth to that of Spirit or super-physical energy, so that once again, the Earth can take it's rightful place in Heaven and mankind can once again stand amongst the gods.

THE ASCENSION OF THE EARTH

If the Earth is removed from it's present position, in space-time, it will be shifted out of a third dimensional zone of density. If it is relocated in a fifth dimensional zone, it would be ascended from the third to the fifth dimension. This, I believe, is how the ascension of the Earth will occur.

Do not allow talk of mass extinction and massive Earth changes alarm you. If you make your spiritual evolvement and service your priority then you can relax and trust what happens to you, to your family and to the world.

"Seek you first the Kingdom of God and his righteousness and everything else will be added unto you."

(Matthew 6:33)

Chapter Ten
Mass Landings & Ascension

Over the last seven years channelled messages have asked us to prepare for three waves of ascension and a mass evacuation of the Earth and then more recently to make ready for mass landings of extra-terrestrials. Most people are left wondering what to believe - especially when predictions never seem to occur within any given time frame.

I believe that ascension and evacuation of the Earth, along the lines of the original ascension message will only occur if and when it has to. As Sananda said, in the Eric Klein channellings

"Ascension will occur at the last possible moment to give the maximum number of people the opportunity to hear about it and prepare themselves"

I am of the opinion that ascension and evacuation would have been necessary had the Gulf War or Balkans crisis escalated into nuclear conflict. The urgency of the 1990/91 channellings reflected the danger posed by the Gulf War and the prediction of the ascension waves beginning by 1995 were based, I am sure, on the great likelihood that the Nato bombing of the Serbs in that year would have drawn Russia and America into a Third World War - with nuclear exchanges predicted to occur in 1999.

Because of the lightwork, prayers, meditations, affirmations - especially the *Affirmation for Russia* enacted in 1994 - and the overall change of consciousness of humanity, the Third World War never happened. I believe that the danger of nuclear war has passed into history so it may no longer be necessary to evacuate the Earth in that eventuality. That is good news for everyone except prophets like me! The object of the prophet is to be proved wrong because his warnings to avert a disaster are heeded. However, should that occur then, he has to deal with the anger and disappointment of those who were expecting his dramatic prophecies to happen.

The latest wave of predictions have been about mass landings of extra-terrestrials. I believe that these are the foreseeing the experience of people on Earth in the eventuality of evacuation not happening prior to the predicted planetary ascension.

I believe that though nuclear war has been averted the predicted Earth changes are still due to occur. These are necessary to the restructuring and cleansing of the Earth prior to her ascension. During the changes, many people unprepared for ascension will die but I am also certain that many destined and ready to ascend will be ascended at that time. Some will also survive and amongst these many could be destined to ascend with the Earth.

Imagine the situation. If you disappear relative to the Earth you will know you have ascended, but if you ascend with the Earth, you will only know it has happened because suddenly the fifth dimension will appear all around you. To you it will seem that fifth-dimensional beings have landed on Earth when in reality it will be you and the Earth that has landed in the fifth dimension. The planetary population of the Earth, at the time of her ascension, would be mass landing in the extra-terrestrial's world. They would not be mass landing on the Earth. However, because of relativity, it would 'appear' that they had mass landed. Whether humanity lands in the fifth dimension or fifth-dimensional beings land in the third dimension, the result is much the same.

There is a great danger in getting caught up in information about the coming changes when in truth we can not really comprehend what is going to happen to us and the Earth in the ascension. We can only work with metaphors and models and in our preoccupation with how and when it will happen we are liable to miss the whole point of ascension. With ascension, the object of the exercise is to get out of the head and into the heart. If we get caught up in the information we are liable to miss the inspiration. It really doesn't matter what happens if we are breathing consciously as we go about our daily lives. If we take the opportunity to think and act with care and loving kindness, if we spread joy and enlightenment, hope and encouragement along every step of our way ascension will happen for us and it won't matter to us when or how.

Ascension is a way not an end. it is the way of the saint and sage, the Yogi and the Mystic. It is the way of the Tao and Zen. It was taught by Krishna and Christ, Buddha and Kabir, Francis of Assisi and every other enlightened master that has ever walked and taught on Earth.

It is the way of surrender and trust, the way of love and courage. It is achieved by taking time to reach the divine in that still quiet space within. It is achieved by dedication to the enlightenment and upliftment of Self and humanity at every given opportunity. It is achieved by inspired communication and networking transcendental information. It is achieved by our being the blissful divine beings that we truly are.

Ascension is not about something that is going to happen in the future sometime. Ascension is about being physical immortals right now. Now is the opportunity to fully physicalise our divinity. Now is the time to be truly sublime. Now is the time to manifest mastery. There are people living on breath. These are people healing and working miracles. Millions are awakening to their Christ Consciousness. The ascension is happening all around us. We are in the quantum leap right now. So my advice is: seek not so much for information as for integration, seek not after the latest news but after the knowledge of your own divine Self where the *real* news lies.

Teachers like me cannot teach you anything new, we can only remind you of what you already know. I spread information to stimulate and awaken and encourage people to keep on the path of ascension. My science and theology, metaphysics and music are platforms from whence I can reach out to the human heart and cry for it to awaken. "Wake up, wake up, for heaven's sake: the time is now". If you are awake then stay in your joy because your deliverance is at hand.

There will be changes on the Earth. The old order has to give way to the new. But we are here to smooth the transition by holding true to our centre and allowing the Spirit to shine through. The heart is the doorway to heaven. The breath leads I AM consciousness through the inner pearly gates into the Kingdom of Heaven within.

It doesn't matter then if 'ascension waves go or the mass landings come' because in that state of surrender to the inner divine Self we are ascended now. There will be no death for us if we are destined for ascension so we are physical immortals right now!

So be ready for anything by being true to yourself. Do whatever makes your heart sing. Follow your joy. Stay really alive. Do whatever is appropriate to each moment as it arrives. Care for yourself and others unconditionally. Don't burden others with your judgements and criticism. *The wise do not criticise*.

Be ever vigilant, ever conscious and ever prepared then if the doorway of ascension, the opening of light appears before you, you will step into it without hesitation. If the extra-terrestrials land you will welcome them with open arms and if neither of these things happen you will continue as the divine Descended Master that you are right now, healing, teaching and inspiring others wherever you go.

So fear not for the future. We have survived the past, we are right in the present and the future will look after itself. Riches are where the heart lies, not in money or material things. Health is in the peaceful heart, not the body beautiful; though all these things matter, the priority is our peace, harmony and well-being in this moment, right now.

> *So don't squander life's precious moments,*
> *Keep searching until you find,*
> *In the breath that leads to Heaven*
> *The source of your Life Divine.*

Chapter Eleven

Meditations for Ascension

by

Hillary Ravenna

1: Grounding ourselves and anchoring the Light.

The Masters and those in the spiritual realms can do nothing for us or Planet Earth unless we ask, give permission and allow them to act through us. We are the ones who physically live on the Earth, so we have to consciously bring down the energies from the higher realms and anchor them into the physical. Energy = Light = Information.

It is through us, as walking, conscious channels for light, that the Divine Plan can unfold. Our mission on Earth is very simple. To quote Archangel Michael *"Our mission on Earth is to be spontaneous radiators of the Divine that we are."*

It is important when working with the higher energies, that we anchor them fully into the Earth, not only because it makes us more efficient and receptive on the practical, physical level, but it keeps us firmly in our bodies. A lot of people on the spiritual path resemble 'hot air balloons': ready to take off any minute!

They are not actually doing anything useful with the energies.

Here is a simple way to ground yourself and anchor the light:

Stand well balanced with both feet flat on the ground. Relax. Eyes closed. Connect with your breath into the heart chakra.

Visualise the heart chakra (maybe as spinning light) and see light energy coming from the heart chakra, down through the body, through the legs and out the bottom of the feet. From there the light goes right to the centre of the Earth. When you feel well connected with the centre of the Earth, bring your attention back once more to the heart. Now visualise a column of light right up above your head (at least 10 Metres up) and see this light descending through the crown chakra on top of the head and down through the body and all the chakras, until it goes out the bottom of the feet and down into the centre of the Earth. Repeat this a couple of times until you feel you are a clear channel for the light to flow through.

As you go about your day, stay connected with your breath and the vision of light coming in at the top of your head and radiating out through the soles of your feet into the Earth. Connecting with this light is actually connecting with your Higher Spirit Self and grounding the light is a way of bringing the higher self into full incarnation.

2: Grounding through the base chakra

Another effective way to ground quickly is to focus on the base chakra in the pelvic region. See it as spinning red - healthy and vibrant like a spinning ball of red fire. Now see the red coming down the veins in your legs and out of the soles of your feet as red roots growing deep into the ground. You will feel the 'heaviness' in your feet.

Alternatively, especially if you are sitting, you can form a connection between your base chakra and the ground by visualising a strong rod (like a metal bar) linking the base chakra to the Earth, giving an instant solid connection.

Just experiment and use your inner guidance to feel what is best for you in different situations. You can always call on Wotanna for assistance. He walked the Earth plane as a Sioux Medicine man and his speciality is to help us keep our feet firmly planted on the ground.

3: Calling on your Higher Self

Ascension can also be described as descension for it is with the descent of our Higher Selves into our lower bodies that we fulfil our Divinity. This can be done simply by focusing on the breath and literally calling (silently or aloud) on your Higher Self to be fully present in your physical body to guide and inspire you. In the earlier process of grounding the light, you were calling on your Higher Self as you visualised it's descent into the physical body as a column of light. You can also visualise the descent of the Higher Self as a golden pyramid of light, large enough to come down and completely surround you, with a golden floor of light closing under your feet.

Your Higher Self will also give you signals to 'tune in', maybe an urge to stop activities and take time to meditate. Sometimes you may experience a ringing in your ears. Don't worry, its just your Higher Self calling to say "get in touch". Acknowledge the call by going within, stilling the mind and focusing on the breath.

4: Finding your Higher Self Name

Just as we have a name in the physical realm, so our Higher Self has a name in the spirit realms. This is sometimes called the I AM name or Starry Name.

Here is one way to find your name.

Stand well balanced. Eyes closed. Feet flat on the floor. Focus into the breath and allow it to take your attention into the heart chakra, then take these energies right into the centre of the Earth (as for grounding the light).

Now visualise a column of light way up above your head. Stretch up as far as you can and grasp the column of light firmly between your hands. See some silver stars come spiralling down from the light into your crown chakra and down into your body. See some more stars spiral down. Stretching up as far as you can, hold onto the light and pull it slowly and firmly down to cover your crown chakra, then the third eye chakra, the throat chakra and into the heart chakra - then push it right down through the lower chakras and into the centre of the Earth. Stretch up again, this time as far as you can. Grasp the light and as you see the stars spiralling and you start to pull down the light, ask for your higher self name. Then

112

bring the light right down though you to the centre of the Earth.

You may hear a name, you may not. You may hear a sound or part of a name. You may hear music or smell an aroma. It doesn't matter what your experience is. You have registered with the Universe the desire to know your Higher Self name and the information will come in its own perfect time. Remember that it is the first thing you hear that counts, before your mind has a chance to come in and doubt. Repeat the process at other times and more information about your higher self may come through. As multidimensional beings, we have many bodies in many realms of many Universes, so we have many names. If you know one of your starry names you may be able to access another.

Don't forget, the deeper into the Earth we can anchor the light, the higher into the Universe we can reach to pull more light in.

5: Aligning the chakras

We have a number of subtle energy bodies coexisting with the physical body. These can be perceived as the aura energy fields extending out from the physical body. They can also be perceived as chakras, energy vortices located in alignment with the physical body. The main seven chakras are located in the following positions: the crown of the head, the forehead or third eye, the throat, the heart, the solar plexus, the abdomen or sacral, and the pelvic or root chakra. Other chakras, both above and below the body are now being activated due to the more powerful energies coming onto the planet in preparation for

Ascension. We can ensure that all our subtle energy bodies are in alignment by working on our chakras.

We cannot ascend unless all our chakras are aligned and fully operational, not just the higher ones. We don't want to ascend just half a body!

This can be done very quickly by bringing down the light of your Higher Self and seeing it pass through every chakra in turn. Visualise all the chakras in a straight line from head to toe. As the light passes through, it cleanses each chakra leaving the colour vibrant and sparkling, radiant and healthy, a spinning vortex of light.

6: Expanding the aura

This is another way to align the chakras and it is very powerful but it does take a little longer. It is wonderful for expanding the aura and accessing higher dimensions.

First connect with the heart chakra through the breath and anchor the light into the centre of the Earth. This visualisation needs to be done quite slowly so that you are only moving on to the next step when you really feel comfortable to do so.

Focus on your breath and establish quiet rhythmic breathing. Be aware of your heart chakra and allow it to expand with every breath you take. Let it expand until it is large enough to overlap the chakras in the throat and solar plexus. Now see these three chakras as one large chakra ever-expanding with every rhythmic breath you take. This chakra expands even more in a huge circle to embrace the third eye chakra and sacral chakra.

Gradually expand again to merge with the crown chakra and the root chakra, and feel your aura really swelling outwards. Keep expanding with your breathing, at the same time taking in more chakras from above and below the body. There are about seven each way, but you may not envelope them all. You will know what is right for you. When you finally experience yourself as one huge chakra just enjoy your breath and your new expanded self.

Don't forget to close down the chakras and protect your aura at the end of your meditation.

7: Lotus Flower Meditation

This meditation is good for:

- Opening and aligning the chakras
- Creating a sacred space
- Bringing group energies into focus
- Personal and planetary healing

Sit comfortably, feet flat on the floor (not crossed), relax, eyes closed. Let your attention go into the breath and just be aware of it rising and falling. You don't have to breathe in any special way, just be comfortable.

As you relax, be aware of the quality behind your breath. It is a feeling of peace, well-being, contentment, fulfilment or fullness. As you breathe out your tensions let them go into the violet flames of St.Germain to be transmuted.

Now take your attention to your crown chakra on top of your head. Visualise there a lotus flower, a thousand petalled lotus flower and it is pale pink. In your own time see the petals of the flower opening up, one by one, until the whole flower has opened wide. Now from way above your head (more than 10 metres above your head) see a column of white light descending until it comes into your crown chakra through the centre of the lotus flower.

Now slowly, in your own time, allow this beautiful light of the Creator to come further into your body. See your third eye chakra opening as a flower and flooding with light. Then the throat chakra opens as a flower and fills with light. And so with all your chakras until they are all open and fully aligned and overflowing with love and light and eventually the light is going right through the bottom of your feet and into the centre of the Earth.

Take time to allow the light to penetrate every cell of your body - revitalising and rejuvenating you completely, all your organs and limbs, your muscles, every blood cell - see them all healthy and vibrant. Allow the light to dissolve any 'sticky' areas of negativity or darkness you may find there.

Now see an opening in the solar plexus, just above the navel, where the light is coming out of your body and filling up your aura, so that eventually you are surrounded by an auric egg of white light.

If you are meditating in a group, allow your aura to expand out on either side of you to embrace the auras of the people next to you. Now see it expand

116

even further until eventually it has embraced everyone in the room and you are all in a single bubble of light.

You have created a sacred space, and into this space you can call on the presence of the Masters of the Ascended Realms of the Great White Brotherhood, who would like to join you. You can specify which ones if you wish. Also at this point, call upon your Higher Self to be fully present in your body and any spirit guides and helpers you would like to be present, to work energetically with you whilst you meditate.

7a: Higher Chakra Meditation

By meditating on the higher chakras we are automatically connecting with our higher subtle energy bodies. The heart chakra connects us to our 5th.dimensional light body whilst our throat, third eye and crown chakras connect us to the 6th., 7th. and 8th. levels of the Universe.

In meditation, it is *where* you place your attention that counts. The simple focus on the breath takes your attention into the heart chakra which connects your consciousness into the fifth dimension.

Lift your tongue into the palate of your mouth and allow this simple action to take your attention into the throat chakra. As you taste the nectar of the throat chakra energy, or as you feel it as a tingling around the edge of your tongue, your consciousness will be lifted into the sixth dimension.

Focus on the light inside your head to bring your attention into the third eye position. As you see the divine light, your consciousness will be taken up into the seventh dimension.

Listen to the sounds inside your head and allow them to lift your attention into the crown chakra. Even if it is just a ringing in your ears, this will bring your consciousness into the eighth dimension of the Universe. As you direct your senses of feeling, tasting, seeing and hearing inwards, you direct your consciousness from the outer physical world into the inner world of spirit.

This is a very simple but powerful meditation as focus on the heart and throat chakras can maintain your connection with your Higher Spirit Self throughout the day.

7b: Personal and Planetary Healing

If there is someone you feel would benefit from healing (on any level, be it physical, emotional, mental or spiritual) simply visualise that person standing under a shower of golden-white light. See them healthy and happy and really dancing in the light, and send the love of the Creator to them. Always be detached from the healing process and allow highest wisdom to dictate the results. Remember that you can call on the Masters to help, especially Sananda.

For planetary healing, use the bubble of light created earlier. Call on the Masters (especially the Blessed Mother Mary) to go with the energy around the world and use it to heal the Earth. See the bubble expand to cover the area where you live, and allow the love and light to shower down to cover your homes. See the bubble expand further to cover the whole country and again pause for a moment for the light to shower down. Gradually see the bubble swell big enough to encircle the Earth. Let yourself be intuitively drawn to any country which needs help at this time, and see the love of the Creator pour down upon it.

When you feel the process is complete, leave the Planet encircled in light, pull yourself back into your own aura and when you are ready to come out of meditation, go down through the chakras closing them down.

7c: Closing down the chakras

At the end of meditation, or any process which involves working with the chakras (or indeed if you are just going 'out into the world' and need some protection), it is vital to close down the chakras one by one and protect your aura. You can do this by seeing each chakra as a flower, close it up, and put a white circle around it with a cross in the middle. When all chakras are protected, finish by protecting your aura, again with a circle of white with a white cross in the middle. You can also use the blue mantle of St.Michael and the blessed Mother Mary to completely surround your aura as you go about your day.

Make sure you are completely back in your body by wriggling your toes, dancing around if necessary, and maybe quickly grounding yourself from the base chakra. Dancing is a wonderful way to get our energies flowing and move the energy blocks. Movement helps the Divine to anchor into the physical body. Joyful movement helps to ground the light.

8: Using the Violet Flame of St.Germain

Besides being on the planet to consciously anchor the light of the Universe, we can also see the Earth as a schoolhouse, and one of the big lessons we are learning is on mastering the emotions. The denseness and negativity here has been very strong, and the Masters are giving us all the help they can to transmute these energies. St.Germain works with the violet flame, and can be called upon at any time to clear negative energies either from within our body or a particular place. If you feel there is some emotion in your body which needs clearing, simply call on St.Germain and visualise yourself completely surrounded by violet flames. See them swirling all around you and inside you. Ask for the emotional energy to be transmuted.

This transmutation process is also good for groups, especially before meditation. If you are accustomed to relaxing by 'breathing out all your worries and tensions', next time breathe them into the violet flames to be transmuted. Don't leave them floating around in the ethers for other people to pick up! If there is some emotion which is a particular problem to you, let it come up, acknowledge it (let it have its say if necessary), thank it for the part it has played in your life, but let it go. Now is the time for it to move on. Direct it into the violet flames. If necessary see yourself putting it into the flames for transmutation as you let it go.

Use this process at any time, anywhere and on anybody. Thank St.Germain for his love and support.

9: Archangel Michael and His Blue Sword

Over years and lifetimes we have built up connections with people, places and things. Even though we may not be physically in touch with these, the connections or ties we have on an etheric level can be very strong. These ties bind us and keep us trapped in the physical plane of reality. The irony is that we need to free ourselves from any attachment to the physical plane so that we can fully enjoy being divinely here.

Recognising problem areas and dealing with them is a must for Ascension. Call on St.Michael with his blue sword to help you. His speciality is cutting the ties that bind. Literally ask him to cut the ties that bind you to a particular problem area. Just relax into the breath and allow him time to work on you energetically. It takes a long time to build up these ties, so they may not disappear all at once. You may have to repeat the process again, but gradually the ties will become weaker until they sever completely. You may find that once you start on the Ascension path, lots of incidents and people will come to mind where you have had a connection in the past or in the present. Just acknowledge them, thank them for the part they have played in your evolution, and let them go as you ask St.Michael to cut you free from each other.

Once that 'sticky' emotional tie is gone, it's much easier to connect with the same people on a higher level. Michael also offers us the protection of his blue mantle. Simply visualise your aura covered in blue and ask for St.Michael's protection in your day or night.

Thank St.Michael for his love, support and protection.

10: I AM Decrees

The Blessed Mother Mary, Sananda the Christ and many other Masters are speaking to us now through our Higher Selves. We can learn to tune into their energies and the guidance they have for us. They are insistent, in all their communications, that we realise what Divine beings we truly are and now we should step into our power and create the world in which we wish to live. To help us do this they advise the use of I AM decrees.

An I AM decree is actually a statement to the Universe which will become manifest if said three times (once for each of our lower bodies, our etheric, emotional and mental bodies).

Sananda recommends the following:

I AM Light
I AM Love
I and the Father AM One
I AM THAT I AM

St.Germaine recommends:

I AM the fullness of my Divine Being in its infinite glorious manifestation.

St.Michael recommends:

I AM a spontaneous radiator of the Divine THAT I AM

It is also recommended that you use your own decrees for personal empowerment e.g.

I AM healthy
    I AM enjoying the abundance of the Universe

These decrees are further empowered if first we state "By the Mighty I AM THAT I AM I decree......" and finish the decree with "I give thanks that it is done".

As more powerful energies come onto the planet it will be much easier to create our own world, our own reality, so be careful what you think. It might just manifest!

For too long now we have looked to others for guidance. We have given our power to religions and governments, experts and people in authority. We have allowed others to take decisions for us, telling us what to do. The time is now for each and everyone of us to step into our own power and rely on the guidance of our Higher Selves.

Let us wholeheartedly embrace this New Age which is now upon us. Ascension is our birthright. All we have to do is let go and allow it to occur.

11 Mudra Meditation (David Ash)

Close the thumbs and forefingers in the classic Mudra for meditation. Relax. Point the tip of the tongue toward the palate and taste the 'light' around the edge of the tongue.

Breathe in for a count of five to seven. Hold the breath for the same count. Expire for the same. Hold the expiration for the same duration. Change the finger Mudra so that the thumbs are closed on the middle fingers. Repeat the breath sequence. Then change the Mudra so that the thumbs and ring fingers are closed. Repeat the 'square' breath sequence. Do it again with the thumbs closed on the little fingers. Reverse the procedure back to the index fingers again so you have done seven finger mudras - one for each chakra - and seven cycles of square breathing.

Relax and breathe normally. You can repeat this procedure as often as you like.

The deep 'square' breathing opens the heart chakra. The fingers align the subtle energy patterns of the body. The tongue, like a pyramid, directs liquid light from the heart, through the throat chakra, into the pineal gland. Close your eyes and indulge in the light of the third eye chakra whilst you drink deep from the spring of life:

Somewhere hidden deep in every human heart,
Lies the spring of Life, the eternal spark,
The door to Heaven stands open wide,
The door is in the heart, so step inside,
Step within the breath you breathe
Breathe in deep now and feel the peace.
Let not your troubles hold you in their sway,
Nor let your problems sweep you away,
These are just the trials that make us strong,
They'll keep on coming whilst to the Earth we belong.
Breathe your way through every trial and task,
Knowing that none will ever last,
And breathe into every good fortune and joy,
Knowing also that they will pass,
Our lessons they come in light and dark
Let neither trick you from your eternal spark
Good and evil are but the masks
That Life wears in the play of the human hearts.

Tailpieces

ASCENSION AND THE GHOST DANCE

Sananda first came with the Ascension Message to the West Coast of America in 1890, when the Native American prophet Kicking Bird had a vision. He said the *one who was pinned to a tree and pierced with a lance by the white man* came to him in Native dress. In the vision, Kicking Bird was asked to take a message out to all the nations of the Native people. They were asked to fast and dance for a year. The dance came to be known as the "Ghost Dance". Kicking Bird was told that after 'a season' the Ghost Dancers would be lifted off the Earth whilst the Earth was cleansed of White Man's civilisation by a whirlwind, then the people would be returned to an Earth which would be re-created anew. The streams would run pure and clean again. The game would be back on the plains and the forests would be as they were before the white man came.

Kicking Bird travelled all over America and the Ghost Dance 'caught on like wild-fire' amongst the Native people. Taken as an act of defiance, the dance was prohibited by the whites but the Indians danced on. The result is history. Men, women and children were massacred at Wounded Knee.

'The Season' spoken of by Sananda - Jesus Christ - when he first appeared to Kicking Bird, was obviously a century because in 1990 Sananda came in channelling to the Californian, Eric Klein, with much the same message of lifting, cleansing and

125

return of those who love and care for the Earth, after it is cleared of the civilisation that is destroying the planet.

Higher-Self

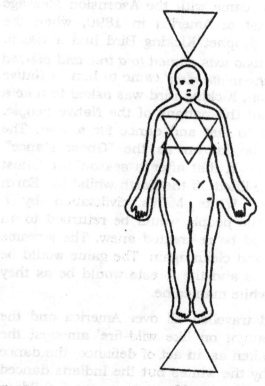

Lower-Self

Ascension involves the integration of the higher and lower self in the heart of the human being.

A little-known aspect of the Ghost Dance is that the Ghost Dancers danced into incarnation in the white races. This explains why so many white people who are drawn to ascension are also attracted to Native American traditions and Medicine Wheel teachings. We are the Ghost Dancers, here to fulfil the Ghost Dance predictions.

THE BIBLE CODE

In his new book, *The Bible Code*, Michael Drosnin reports that there is a hidden code in the Hebrew version of the Bible which has just been cracked by computer. Every significant event in history is detailed in this code along with names, places and dates.

According to Drosnin, it was encoded in the Bible that an atomic holocaust was to occur as a result of nuclear terrorism against Israel. The date given was 1996. This vindicates the Ascension message. the original date given for the beginning of the ascension waves was 1996. This was obviously in preparation for the nuclear conflagration anticipated for 1996.

The word "delayed" was discovered beside the 1996 warning. Two more dates have been given for the possibility of an atomic holocaust; 2000 and 2006. This latter date fits with channelled messages from the Blessed Mother Mary, that through grace, we have been given an extra ten years to prepare for the end.

The world is teetering on the edge of a precipice because of the danger of nuclear terrorism. Nuclear devices from Russia have passed into the hands of small nations, and terrorist groups. This is a fact of life. *The Bible Code* makes it clear that the danger facing the world is the threat of nuclear terrorism - primarily against Israel.

It is easy to dismiss the Ascension message but the fact is, we are living on a time bomb. We are fortunate that a plan of salvation has been offered to us. Those who ignore it or dismiss it may find themselves left to their own devices on the Earth, attempting to survive the aftermath of a nuclear holocaust and the 'Great Earthquake' which, according to The Bible Code, is due to occur at the same time. The Bible Code makes it clear that these disasters can be averted. the choice is up to us.

PRANIC NUTRITION

As an individual attains to self-mastery on the path of ascension it becomes possible for them to relinquish their attachment to food, and be sustained instead on Prana.

Prana is the energy of Life. It is the 'chi' of acupuncture, orgone energy or odic force and, in my own science, the super-energy of the etheric field. Sources of prana are fresh vegetables, sprouting grains and seeds, and fresh fruit. However the main source of prana for each individual is in the breath.

A number of people in the ascension movement have chosen to live entirely on prana derived from the breath. One of these is the Australian facilitator Jasmuheen who has lived since 1993 without food.

In her book Prana and Immortality: Living on Light Jasmuheen describes the 21-day process she went through to "kick the eating habit". However, since then she has pioneered a new technique for coming off food and onto prana. As she explained to me:

Each one of us has a Body Elemental, the spirit that is responsible for the welfare of the etheric and physical bodies. The Jasmuheen system entails commanding the Body Elemental to derive sustenance from prana instead of food. It is very simple, first call forth the Body Elemental as follows:

"I call on the presence of my Body Elemental"

Imagine the Elemental as a private soldier, standing in front of you, the General, awaiting orders. You then command it as follows:

"Elemental Spirit of my body, I command, from this moment forward, that you derive the nourishment required to maintain my body in peak physical health from the pranic forces. If I eat anything, it is for sociality and sense gratification and not nutrition. You are to absorb the vitamins and minerals, fats, carbohydrates, proteins and water that I require to be balanced and healthy at ......Kg. (here program your Elemental Computer to the optimum weight you wish to maintain) from the ethers. You may derive prana from fruit and vegetables that I take as bulk. So be it." (I have modified Jasmuheen's system to include fruit and raw salad vegetables should you choose to eat them for prana, and bulk to maintain healthy bowel movements.)

After this programming of your body elemental, trust the process and listen to your body voice. Your body will tell you what you need. You can eat anything you like for pleasure. This system is not a fast or a food fad. It is a way to attain freedom from the need or addiction to food. It may be important on social occasions to eat food that is given to you. That is fine. Enjoy what you are given but also enjoy the freedom from having to go out and get food. Once you are on Pranic Nutrition you will have no further need to buy, cook and eat food. You will do all that only when it is a pleasure not a task. This is a way of self-mastery, not self-denial.

I recommend the 21-day program that Jasmu-heen did because it is worthwhile process and a demonstration to yourself that you can live entirely off pranic energy - you will need a period on retreat for this. Also the 21-day process was channelled by the Masters and should be done if you want to live entirely on prana. However, I have opted for the gentle transition of eating less junk food and a lot more fruit and salad as a movement toward full Pranic Nutrition. Fruit and salad are a valid form of Pranic Nutrition - especially if you choose **not** to do the 21-day fast. Your body will tell you from day to day what you need. It is your intent that counts. If it is your intent to subsist entirely off liquid light, all your dietary needs will precipitate from the etheric body into every cell of your physical body.

If you want to enjoy eating - as I do - choosing to eat live rather than dead food will lead to good health, long life and lack of disease. Pranic Nutrition leads to a new level of sensitivity, far more energy, freedom from disease and abundant health, optimum weight (you program your body for the weight you have always wanted) a reduction in your need for sleep, and more disposable income, and time saved in shopping and cooking. Living mainly on fruit and salad you will attain great benefit both spiritually and physically.

The way of Pranic nutrition is the way of freedom. Tantalise your taste buds with whatever you fancy, now and again and do not become a food fad or a social outcast. Ascension doesn't depend on nutrition but Jasmuheen's system offers an opportunity to change your attitude and overcome your addiction to food and drinks (alcoholic and non-alcoholic) and take a major step in the attainment of self-mastery on your ascension path.

EMBRACE IMMORTALITY

Are you addicted to death? Do you really want to go on reincarnating? Do you relish the idea of starting all over again in another body, being a baby, going to school, painstakingly rediscovering everything you have learnt in this amazing lifetime? Are you even certain there will be the opportunity to re-incarnate again on the Earth?

We are being offered immortality. Eternal life is ours for the taking. We can keep the lessons we have learnt in this lifetime and not lose everything we have learnt in the loss of consciousness called death. But do we love ourselves enough to live with ourselves forever? Do we really want to be immortal? If Yes:

Let go to love, for yourself and for all others alive on the Earth. Let go of your attachment to death. Surrender your limiting beliefs - especially that you have to die. Release all the negativity in your thoughts and emotions. Let go of your guilt, shame and judgements. Love yourself and others unconditionally. You and they are fine. Everything is working itself out perfectly. The Universe is OK It does what it does only to teach you and me lessons so that we can come into self-mastery and embrace immortality.

INTEGRATION FOR ASCENSION

Ascension involves the integration of the higher and the lower self in the heart of the human being. This is represented by the 'Star of David'. An aspiration of divinity is to be fully incarnate on matter. The chosen vehicle for this is the hu(god)-man being. This is achieved by the descent of the higher spirit- self. An aspiration of soul is to ascend into spirit. This is achieved by the ascent of lower soul-self. The higher and lower selves meet and merge in the heart. Their fusion occurs through love in the heart chakra. This is the integration for ascension.

It is crucial, at this time, that we fully integrate our higher spirit-selves into physical embodiment, to prepare the body and soul for the ascension into the realms of spirit - the fifth dimension (accessed via the breath through the heart chakra) and beyond. This integration will also enable us to operate effectively as divine beings whilst we are on the Earth. Ascension isn't so much about leaving the Earth - apart from the possibility of a temporary evacuation whilst she is cleansed prior to her own transition into the fifth dimension - as about being able to remain with the Earth after her ascension into glory. Ascension is for integrated, compassionate beings, who wish to transcend death and enjoy the freedom to come and go to the Earth - after her ascension - as they choose.

RECONCILIATION FOR ASCENSION

The ascension is the reconciliation between light (spirit) and dark (matter). This is also represented by the 'Star of David' and demonstrated by Sananda in his incarnation as Jesus Christ. He represented the highest level of spirit descending into matter. In his life and death he brought about a reconciliation of the good and evil in man, and paved the way for our resurrection and ascension. Prior to our recreation and ascension we need to find, within ourselves, reconciliation of the duality of good and evil. We cannot ignore the shadow, we have to acknowledge it without fear and let it go in love. Only then will there be healing in every heart and home, every family, community and nation on Earth. We can intend this for our future in the *Affirmation for the Millennium*.

AFFIRMATION FOR THE MILLENNIUM

By the Mighty
I AM THAT I AM
I affirm that love and light,
joy and laughter, peace, truth
and highest wisdom prevail in me
and humanity and that healing occur
in every heart and home, in every
family, community and nation
on Earth, and the duality
of good and evil be
reconciled now
and forever.

Please repeat this decree 34 times a day, for at least 34 consecutive days, in preparation for the millennium and encourage others to do so too. It is more powerful if said out loud with feeling and intent and if it is repeated in groups of three or more.

If you make up a rosary of 34 beads, this will help you to keep count and the beads in your pocket will remind you each day to make the affirmation until it becomes an integral part of your daily routine. Complete the affirmation with a few minutes of feeling with your breath into the place of peace in your heart.

The number 34 is chosen because 33.33 is perhaps the most powerful sacred number. Affirmations repeated 34 times are very effective. Repeated for 34 consecutive days makes them unbelievably effective. In groups of 3 they are even more powerful. A group of 34 people, repeating an affirmation such as this, 34 times a day for 34 days, could shift the Universe.

An affirmation such as this, invoked globally, has the power to save the Earth and the human race from conflict and destruction. This affirmation will set the scene for the resolution of many problems that confront us and help to bring in the long awaited millennium of peace and enlightenment, joy and celebration that has been predicted for this time. If you don't like the wording, change it and say it as you like. What matters is the global unity of intent as together we affirm our future! The greatest force in the world is people in joy, love and laughter, people in their power, people networking, healing and working for the whole out of compassion for all. We have the power to heal ourselves, others and the Earth. Please enact and network the *Affirmation for the Millennium*

AFFIRMATION FOR RUSSIA

The Blessed Mother Mary has called for prayer for Russia and world peace. To bring about peace, harmony and light in Russia and throughout the world, individuals and groups have been repeating the following decree, since 1994, on a daily basis:

I command that Love, Light, Peace and highest wisdom prevail in Russia and throughout the world, and war be banished from the Earth forever: I AM THAT I AM!

Please include this decree for peace in your daily practice of prayer and meditation. Repeat it three times at least. Many people have repeated it 34 times a day for 34 days to enact the sacred number of 33.3. In "The Only Planet of Choice" (Gateway Books 1993) we are told that this number is the most powerful for enacting intentions.

After this decree was enacted 34 times a day for 34 days in Lent 1994, by individuals throughout the world, and then by groups of 34 people on Good Friday - in honour of the 33.3 years of Jesus' life on Earth - peace has come to the Middle East, South Africa, Northern Ireland and the Balklands.

If you decide to work with this enactment for peace, a string or circle of 34 beads will help you to maintain count. and if you wish to pray for another country, replace 'Russia' with any other country name of your choice.

DAILY AFFIRMATIONS

Here are a selection of daily affirmations to use with your 34 beads. I recommend them to people on the Ascension path. The first is an I Am affirmation:

By the I Am that I Am,

May my living be sacred,

By the I Am that I am,

May my loving be true,

By the I am that I am,

May my longing unite me,

With the Mighty I Am that I Am.

I work with the Mother Mary as my personal 'Master Guide' The prayer below is important to me:

Blessed Mother Mary, By your Immaculate Conception, purify my body, inspire my mind and sanctify my soul that I may better serve the heavenly, Father in fulfilment of the divine plan on Earth.

I also work with the Goddess energy in the form of Quan Yin. My prayer to her is sweet and simple:

Sweet Quan Yin, merge me in the ecstasy of true love, that I may know that which is truly divine.

It is important that we are grateful for Life:

May our loving be sacred, our passion be prayer and our time be a blessing with those who care. And for the gift of life we give heartfelt thanks to the creator in Heaven and Blessed Mother Earth

This prayer to the Great Spirit is an affirmation for personal and planetary ascension:

Come Great Spirit, fill the hearts of we your people, enkindle within us the fire of your love. Come forth Great Spirit that we may be recreated, and thou shalt renew the face of the Earth.

THE PLANETARY GRID SYSTEM

The face of the Earth needs to be renewed. It has been thrown out of balance with the disruption of the ley-line system, due the expansion of roads, drilling, quarrying, industrial and urban development. Negative energies accumulate in huge cities and industrial complexes.

A new temporary grid system has come into being. We are it. We are the nervous system of Mother Earth.

As Workers of the Light, we are creating an energetic grid system which is covering the planet and bringing her back into balance. Each light worker represents a node in the grid. As each one of us anchors the light we activate the grid and through our networking we spread it further afield.

At present only the Western half of the planetary grid system is well activated. There is an urgent need to activate the Eastern half and the Masters have indicated that this can be achieved through Russia and her neighbouring countries. As each person consciously works with the Light, sending it into the Earth and radiating it to others, we create a strong network through which Divine energy can flow.

You can help. Everyone of us can help. Every single one of us counts. As we go about our daily lives - whether we're walking the dog, doing the gardening, working in the office or playing with the baby in the park, we can be a Star and shine with God's Love and Light in this world. Please send love, light and support to Russia and the Eastern nations of the Earth. They need practical help in the form of books and tapes and letters of encouragement. Why not twin with a lightworker in the East and support them in their efforts to establish the ascension network and planetary grid in their part of the world.

Wake Up! Be Conscious! The Time is Now!

Songs for Ascension

GARLAND OF LOVE

With every beat of the human heart,
There's the purest drop of love,
To bind every human heart into a garland,
Of love to stretch the world around,
Oh a garland of love to stretch the world around.

With every ebb and flood of tide,
There's a hope for the world,
To survive the darkest time in all the ages,
If only we could find our drop of love,
Oh if everyone could find their drop of love.

With every breath that comes and goes,
There's a treasure beyond,
All things we can see and touch with this human
frame, if only we can search our hearts within,
Oh if only everyone can search their hearts within.

With every beat of the human heart,
There's the purest drop of love,
To bind every human heart into a garland,
Of love to stretch the world around,
Oh a garland of love to stretch the world around.

David Ash 1981

TAKE THE JOURNEY HOME

Taught to believe that things are the way they seem
We have forgotten the world is but a dream.
Its time to awaken, its time to unlearn
Its time to let go and take the journey home.

Accelerating change is the order of the day
As all human structures begin to fade away.
Its time to awaken, its time to unlearn,
Its time to let go and take the journey home.

Let the heart lead the head, that's the only way.
The mind has to know it no longer holds full sway.
Its time to awaken, its time to unlearn,
Its time to let go and take the journey home.

For long we have wandered the Earth on our own,
Now all of heaven is beckoning us home.
Its time to awaken, its time to unlearn,
Its time to let go and take the journey home.

Take a leap of faith, plunge through the door,
Rise to your glory and bow to death no more.
Its time to awaken, its time to unlearn,
Its time to let go and take the journey home.

Many a lifetime we've waited for this call,
Now we have to choose once and for all.
Its time to awaken, its time to unlearn,
Its time to let go and take the journey home.

Just focus on the breath, that's all we have to do.
Grace will lift us and love will see us through.
Its time to awaken, its time to unlearn,
Its time to let go and take the journey home,
Its time to just flow and take the journey home.

David Ash 1992

PLAN OF AGES

Somewhere hidden deep in every human heart,
Lies the spring of Life, the eternal spark,
The door to Heaven stands open wide,
The door is in the heart, so step inside,
Step within the breath you breathe
Breathe in deep now and feel the peace.

The plan of ages slowly unfolds,
Within its great purpose man evolves,
Ages of suffering grim to bear,
But how else would we learn to love care and share,
So let not your troubles hold you in their sway,
Nor let your problems sweep you away,
These are just the trials that make us strong,
They'll keep on coming whilst to the Earth we belong.

So breathe your way through every trial and task,
Knowing that none will ever last,
And breathe into every good fortune and joy,
Knowing also that they will pass,
Our lessons they come in light and dark
Let neither trick you from your eternal spark
Good and evil are but the masks
That Life wears in the play of the human hearts.

David Ash 1996

REAL STILLNESS

Have you ever let real stillness for a moment be your all, have you ever stopped a moment and lived at all, Have you ever stopped to ponder but never thought at all, have you ever stopped to wonder why ever you were born.

In the bustle of living we never live at all, Our lives may come together but on life we never call, And in every single moment of our lives flying by, There's a wonder all the words ever spoken can't describe.

So busy talking, so busy thinking, so busy toiling for a dime, so busy doing, so busy dying, but when we die we leave behind, all the people, all the money, all the houses all behind, and as the mists of time go swirling, of our lives we've spent our time.

To late to ponder on the meaning and the purpose of this life, to late to see a single dewdrop in the morning sun alight, to late to feel in every moment, such a joy, unending bliss, to late to find the door to heaven, in the heart we left behind.

So don't squander life's precious moments, keep
searching till you find, in the breath that leads to
heaven, the source of your life divine.

David Ash 1977

TIME TO BE HAPPY

Dance on the cliffs with me, dance by the shining sea,
Come lets really live and be happy.
Gone are the days of strife, gone are the nights of
gloom, now is the time to sing and be happy.
Come and laugh with me, sing and be carefree,
It's time to be happy, really really happy.

Run in the woods and fields, run in the morning dew,
So much to find and feel, so much to see and do.
Paddling in the rock pools, falling in a stream or two,
Let the wind and water in and soak right through.
So many stars to count, so much to rejoice about,
So lets be really happy, really really happy.

Let the darkness pass away,
Let the light shine through,
Choose to think thoughts that heal
Not thoughts that make us blue.
The mind will take us back to times,
Of anguish and despair,
Reminding us of love lost and those that didn't care.
But now whilst life is kind and love's not hard to find,
Choose to be happy, in peace and harmony.
Its time to be happy, in joy and laughter
Its time to be happy, really really happy
Its time to be happy.

David Ash 1996

PROPHET OF GOD

Prophet of God, rare indeed,
Travelling far over land and sea,
Speaks to all who will understand,
All he needs is a helping hand.

So listen to what he has to say,
Before he is gone, on his way,
Open your mind then wait and see,
Your heart will tell if its absurdity,
Is he right or is he wrong,
Time will tell, it won't be long.

God has sent His word to mankind,
In every age, to everyone,
But who will stop and harken when,
The messenger comes round again and again.
Prophets have come into this dark time,
With the very last word from God to mankind,
The final choice for everyone,
Whether we want love or destruction.

So listen to what they have to say,
Before they are gone on their way,
Open your mind then wait and see,
You heart will tell if its absurdity,
Are they right or are they wrong,
Time will tell, it won't be long.

David Ash 1996

TIMES OF CHANGE

Times of change for the Earth are here,
Time to let go of the things we hold dear,
Releasing is the process that people most fear,
But let go we must as the end times draw near.
If we let go of our things without fear,

Surrendering hold on those we hold dear,
These things will return to make it quite clear,
That we can trust life, we have nothing to fear.
The god that made us had a great fear,
That man would someday outshine him down here,
So he denied us the tree of life,
And threw us all out into pain death and strife.
For this great sin down God is drawn,
In every baby God is born,
Thus onto Earth God is thrust,
To learn that in life even he must place his trust.
We are the gods here in human form,
Here to overcome through battle pain and storm,
That tenacious hold onto power greed and pride,
Preventing us as gods from evolving on high.
Now this great learning has almost been done,
For many on Earth the battle is won,
With no more pride and nothing left to keep,
We are now ready to take the quantum leap,
Gone is our faith in the Bible and the beer,
Gone is our longing for comfort and good cheer,
Gone is our trust in what we see and hear,
Gone is our trust in our loved ones so dear.
We are the ones with neither friend nor foe,
Ready to surrender everything we know,
We are the ones standing on our own,
Solitary eagles about to soar home.

David Ash 1995

DARKNESS PASSING

Singing in a woodland glade,
Laughing by an ocean wave,
Dancing in the spring sunshine,
Casting out the winter shadows,

Leaving all the rain and storms behind,
Step into a sundrenched morning,
Notice how the birds are calling,
Let the freshest breeze blow through your mind.

Dark of night is passing,
Light breaking in the sky,
Birdsong in full chorus,
Greets the dawn before it,
Turns to crimson clouds on high,
Sun slowly rising,
Red then golden blazing,
Banished is darkness from the day.

Darkest of ages passing,
Dawn of new light for mankind,
Let it blaze before us,
Filling up our hearts with gladness,
Leaving all the fear and shame behind
Taking on a brave new morning,
Following a heart felt calling,
Let the new ideas into your mind,
Let the new ideas into your mind,
Let the new ideas into your mind.

David Ash 1995

LIVING IN THIS MODERN WORLD

Living in this modern world wondering where we are,
Even though we're on the move we're never going far,
And if we never ask the way how will we ever know,
It's so far away we think we have to go,
When all we need to do is just let go,
Allowing life to flow in its own gentle way,
And simply be at peace throughout the day.

Sometime long ago this is the way we were,
We had that real feeling when we had nowhere to go,
We found an inner stillness when we moved really
Slow. Oh where oh where do we go when we're moving
So fast. What do we think that we can grasp,
As our minds are spinning in each hectic day,
We throw the quality away.

So many are alive but so few know how to live,
We have so many things but who knows how to give,
Clinging to what we own we fill our lives with fear,
And the struggle to buy more things is keeping us
Poor, always needing more and more,
Debts keep mounting, the money's gone so fast,
Is this what life is really for.

He with nothing is he with least to lose,
With each day that comes he can do just what he
Choose, when he parted with his things he parted
with His cares. If everyone was giving real abundance
Would be theirs. Hearts light, eyes bright, laughter
Ringing loud and clear, we'd all have given away our
Fears, we would all have given away our fears.

David Ash 1990.

LOVE IS THE ANSWER

Love is the answer,
Love is the hope,
Love is the only thing that can save us in this world,
Love is the key to open up the heart,
Love is the place where life really starts,

But love isn't given with a wedding ring,
Love isn't given when a singer sings,
Love alone from the soul will spring, unexpected,
Unreasoned, usually a fleeting passing thing,

But love, endless love,
In a flood that knows no bounds,
Will gush forth from the soul,
And will sweep the world around,
If the soul is only open like a flower in the spring,
And the mind if it's harnessed,
That wild heartless thing,
And devotion if given with love from the heart,
In an instant we'll be given,
Love, eternal love,
Love, eternal love,
Love, eternal love.

David Ash 1977

THE LOVE OF OUR LORD

The Love of Our Lord,
Makes every moment right,
Makes living worthwhile,
Makes life's burden light.
The Love of Our Lord,
Brings all things to be,
From each spark of life,
To the mighty galaxy.
But the Love of Our Lord,
Within the human heart,
Means more than the world to Our Lord.

The Love of Our Lord,
In the setting of the sun,
In the thunder of the sea,
In the busy honey bee.
The Love of Our Lord,
In the birds flying south,
In the early morning dew,
Makes every moment new.

But the Love of Our Lord,
Within the human heart,
Means more than the world to Our Lord.

The Love of Our Lord,
Means more than all the gold,
More than all the power,
To the priceless human soul.
With the Love of Our Lord,
We have more than a king,
More than this world,
We have everything.
But the Love of Our Lord,
Within the human heart,
Means more than the world to Our Lord.

(David Ash 1977)

THANKSGIVING

Once again as autumn winds are blowing by my
window, once again another season's circle almost
Closed, once again a time to recall how often,
Are we really grateful for what our life has given.

Once again as golden apples fall into the basket,
Misty mornings when fresh mushrooms grace the
Meadow green, when swallows gather as clouds in the
Evening, then for life's banquet, lets give
thanksgiving.

And when the log fire's a'crackling,
And when the howling gale lulls the land to sleep,
And when the lashing rain rattles on your window
Pane, then tell the angels that you're still living.

And then the soft spring sunshine will bring you
Laughter, and then the woodland flowers will dance at
Your feet, because in season, if we give thanks to
God,
God, in His own wise time we will see,
Because in season, if we give thanks to God,
God in His own wise time will set us free.

David Ash 1976

Bibliography

Ambrose David, Miles, Christopher and Watkins, Leslie: **Alternative 3,** *Avon Books* (1979)

Alexandersson, Olaf: **Living Water: Viktor Schauberger and the Secrets of Natural Energy,** *Gateway Books* (1990)

Ash, David & Hewitt, Peter: **The Vortex: Key to Future Science,** *Gateway Books* (1990)

Ash, David: **The New Science of the Spirit,** *The College of Psychic Studies* (1995)

Brinkley, Damien & Paul Perry: **Saved by the Light,** *Piatkus* (1994)

Cooper, William: **Revelations of Awareness,** Special Report 90-2 (1989)

Drosnin, Michael: **The Bible Code,** *Simon & Schuster, New York; Weidenfeld & Nicolson, London, (1997)*

Dutta, Rex: **Flying Saucer Message,** *Pelham Books* (1972)

Good, Timothy: **Above Top Secret,** *Sidgwick & Jackson* (1987)

Helsing, Jan van: **Secret Societies,** *Ewertverlag, PO Box 35290 Playa del Ingles, Gran Canaria, Spain* (1995)

Hoyle, Sir Fred: **The Intelligent Universe,** *Michael Joseph* (1983)

Hurtak, James J.: **The Keys of Enoch,** *The Academy for Future Science* (1973)

Jasmuheen, **Prana and Immortality: Living on Light**

Klein, Eric: **The Crystal Stair & The Inner Door,** *Oughten House* (1992 & 1994)

Lings Martin: **Muhammad: his life based on the earliest sources,** *Islamic Texts Society with George Allen & Unwin* (1983)

Marciniak, Barbara: **Bringers of the Dawn & Earth: Pleiadian Keys to the Living Library,** *Bear & Co* (1992 & 1995)

Marinov, Stefan: **Deutsch Physik,** *East West Publishers* (1992)

Newman, Joseph: **The Energy Machine of Joseph Newman** (1986)

Mascaró Juan: **The Bhagavad Gita,** *Penguin Classics* (1962)

Nichols, Preston: **The Montauk Project,** *Sky Books*, New York (1992)

Schlemmer, P.V.: **The Only Planet of Choice,** *Gateway Books, Bath BA2 8QJ* (1993)

Steiger, Brad & Bielek, Alfred: **The Philadelphia Experiment,** *Inner Light Books*

Stubbs, Tony: **An Ascension Handbook,** *Oughten House* (1991)

Biographies

David Ash is a science graduate of London University. He has worked for many years as a full-time writer and lecturer and travels the world presenting his work. His unique enthusiasm, endearing humour and inspired observations about the nature of the spiritual worlds in the light of science make him a fascinating and uplifting teacher.

Since 1991 he has spoken throughout the U.K. and in Malaysia, Thailand, Cambodia, Australia, New Zealand, Canada, the U.S.A., Spain, Holland, France, Belgium, Germany, Sweden, Denmark, Lithuania, Russia, and South Africa and Zimbabwe. David is the author of "The Vortex: Key To Future Science" (with Peter Hewitt), "The Tower of Truth", "New Science of the Spirit" and "The Two Faces of God."

Hillary Ravenna supported David on his spiritual path for many years and accompanied him on his first trip to Australia where she discovered the now famous Ascension Tapes of Eric Klein. Hillary is a teacher of ascension and meditation in her own right travelling alone to Lithuania and Russia in 1994. She spoke to groups there, appeared on Russian television, and paved the way for David's subsequent visit to Vilnius, St.Petersburg and Moscow.

The Amethyst Group have been channelling and healing in Dawlish, Devon for many years. In 1993, they began to channel Sananda, Ashtar, and Michael of the Ashtar Command. The enclosed Ascension Plan

has been taken from a number of their UK channellings.